BEST RADIO
PLAYS OF 1979

Previous Giles Cooper Award volumes

Pearl by John Arden (Special Award 1978)

Best Radio Plays of 1978

(Richard Harris: *Is It Something I Said?*
Don Haworth: *Episode on a Thursday Evening*
Jill Hyem: *Remember Me*
Tom Mallin: *Halt! Who Goes There?*
Jennifer Phillips: *Daughters of Men*
Fay Weldon: *Polaris*)

BEST RADIO PLAYS OF 1979

The Giles Cooper Award Winners

Shirley Gee: Typhoid Mary
Carey Harrison: I Never Killed My German
Barrie Keeffe: Heaven Scent
John Kirkmorris: Coxcomb
John Peacock: Attard in Retirement
Olwen Wymark: The Child

EYRE METHUEN/BBC PUBLICATIONS

First published in Great Britain in 1980 by Eyre Methuen Ltd
11 New Fetter Lane, London EC4P 4EE and BBC Publications,
35 Marylebone High Street, London W1M 4AA.

Set in IBM Journal by 𝔽 Tek-Art, Croydon, Surrey
Printed in Great Britain by Fakenham Press Ltd, Fakenham, Norfolk

ISBN 0 413 47130 6

CONTENTS

THE GILES COOPER AWARDS: a note on the selection

Giles Cooper
As one of the most original and inventive radio playwrights of the post-war years, Giles Cooper was the author that came most clearly to mind when the BBC and Eyre Methuen were in search of a name when first setting up their jointly sponsored radio drama awards in 1978. Particularly so, as the aim of the awards is precisely to encourage original radio writing by both new and established authors — encouragement in the form both of public acclaim and of publication of their work in book form.

Eligibility
Eligible for the awards was every original radio play first broadcast by the BBC domestic services during 1979 (almost 500 plays in total). Excluded from consideration were translations, adaptations and dramatised 'features'.

Categories
In order to widen the scope of the awards and to ensure that the resulting anthology volume would represent the broad variety of radio playwriting, the judges were asked to select one outstanding play from each of the five Radio 4 drama slots: the Monday Play (usually 90 minutes long), Saturday Night Theatre (90 minutes), Afternoon Theatre (60 minutes), Thirty-Minute Theatre and Just Before Midnight (15 minutes), and one play from Radio 3's drama output (varying in length from 20 to 120 minutes).

Selection
The producer-in-charge of each drama slot was asked to put forward about five or six plays for the judges' consideration. This resulted in a 'short-list' of some 30 plays from which the final selection was made. The judges were entitled to nominate further plays for consideration provided they were eligible. Selection was made on the strength of the script rather than of the production, since it was felt that the awards were primarily for *writing* and that production could unduly enhance or detract from the merits of the original script.

Judges
The judges for the 1979 awards were:
> Martin Esslin, Professor of Drama, Stanford University, California, and ex-head of BBC Radio Drama
> Nicholas Hern, drama editor, Eyre Methuen
> Richard Imison, Script Editor, BBC Radio Drama
> Gillian Reynolds, radio critic, *The Daily Telegraph*

THE MONDAY PLAY
TYPHOID MARY

by Shirley Gee

For Tommy and Harry,
my mother and father,
with my love.

Shirley Gee trained at the Webber-Douglas Academy of Dramatic Art and was an actress until her marriage. Her first play *Stones* was runner-up in the Radio Times Drama Bursary Award and was broadcast in 1974. Then came *The Vet's Daughter* (an adaptation) in 1976, *Moonshine* in 1977, in which Rosemary Leach won Best Actress in the Imperial Tobacco Awards, *Typhoid Mary* and *Bedrock* in 1979. All her plays have been directed by David Spenser. *Typhoid Mary* was a BBC Italia Prize entry for 1979 and received the jury's Special Commendation. It also won the Society of Authors/Pye Award for Best Original Play of 1979. She is married to actor Donald Gee. They have two sons, Joby (13) and Daniel (12) and live in London at Worlds End.

Typhoid Mary was first broadcast on BBC Radio 4 on 15th January 1979. The cast was as follows:

MARY	Margaret Whiting
DR GEORGE SOPER	Daniel Massey
ELLIOT KENDALL	Ed Bishop
MARY as a child	Susan Sheridan
SISTER JOSEPH	Sheila Grant
FATHER JOHN/OTIS	Denys Hawthorne
IMMIGRATION OFFICIAL/TUTOR	Peter Whitman
AGNES	Sandra Dickinson
ELSPETH	Elizabeth Proud
MRS PALMER	Carol Boyd
NURSE RHODES	Helen Horton
NURSE ROBINSON	Nicolette McKenzie
FRANKLYN	Andrew Branch
LANCE	Tim Bentinck
JUDGE	Alan Tilvern
HEALTH DEPARTMENT OFFICIAL	Rod Beacham
O'RORKE	Harry Towb
OTHER PARTS	Susan Sheridan; Sheila Grant; Denys Hawthorne; Peter Whitman; Sandra Dickinson; Elizabeth Proud; Carol Boyd; Helen Horton; Nicolette McKenzie; Andrew Branch; Tim Bentinck; Alan Tilvern; Rod Beacham; John Bull; Brenda Kaye; Jonathan Scott; Ian Hoare; Andrew Bagley; Sarah Bryett; Alison Draper

Director: David Spenser

MARY (*over*). My window has no bars. The days go by. It's
Christmas Day today they said, but I don't know. You can't stick
a sprig of holly on a gas bracket and call it Christmas. I hear the
brown river flowing over bricks and bones and old saucepans. I can
still move my head and watch the sky lighten, first to the grey of a
fish kettle lid, then white like a cod's belly. There's daffodils in a
jar on the sill. He'll have put them there. He's been after me for my
life again. I might throw him a bit of a fact, it's not his fault, I'm
not angry any more, but sometimes when I remember it isn't true
memory. Not always. It's all so long ago. When the others come, I
tell them nothing. I hold my breath as long as I can, I close my
eyes, and I lock my brain, and then they can clatter on like a
sinkful of pots, but they can't reach inside me. I'm something of a
marvel to them, they want to know things, but I don't give a soused
pig's ear for them. They quail very easy, they soon slink off.
Well, I don't think I'll be here much longer. (*Sound of humming
and spoons.*) God bless America, land of the free. What a strange
old time it's been. Locked away from the world for something
I've never done.

*Ireland 1880. Sweet Molly Malone hummed by a drunken street singer
tapping and playing spoons — mix into children's voices.*

CHILDREN. Ring a ring a roses
   a pocket full of posies
   a tishoo a tishoo
   we all fall DOWN.

   Laughter. They chant it again.

FIRST CHILD. Not her. Not her. Don't let her in.

SECOND CHILD. Go off away, Molly Malone.

MARY. Why? Why can I not play?

SECOND CHILD. Because you stink of fish.

FIRST CHILD. You're too fat.

THIRD CHILD. Twice round the churchyard, once round Mary.

ALL. Twice round the churchyard, once round Mary, twice round the churchyard, once round Mary.

SECOND CHILD. Her father's so much beer in him he squelches when he walks.

FIRST CHILD. Her cottage smells.

MARY. It doesn't. It doesn't.

FIRST CHILD. It does so. It smells of old knickers.

SECOND CHILD. Her mother dries her knickers on the oven door.

THIRD CHILD. Old knicker Mary, old knicker Mary.

ALL. Old knicker Mary, old knicker Mary.

MARY. She doesn't, she doesn't, I'll kill you.

SECOND CHILD. Fish fish fish, Molly stinks of fish.

ALL. Fish fish fish, Molly stinks of fish.

MARY. I can't help it, it's working on the stall.

FIRST CHILD. Don't sit next to me, Molly, dinner time, do me a kindness, don't sit by me.

SECOND CHILD. She has taties and rats for dinner. Taties and rats.

MARY. Stop it. It's not my fault. Stop it. I'll kill you all, you wait, I'll kill you.

Scuffling. Laughter. Crying.

SISTER. Children! (*The noise dies fast.*) It's the strap for anyone not in their place, bolt upright, silent as bones, before I count to ten. One. Two. Three. Four. Mother of God, Mary Malone, what are you doing here. Were you not told to keep away? Go over to the doorway now. Open the door. Keep your distance. Whatever possessed you to come today?

MARY. It's Monday, Sister. And I've the Kings of Ireland learned, right through, without a one in the wrong place.

SISTER. Keep in the doorway. Is the baby bad?

MARY. We don't know which way he intends to take, Sister.

SISTER. Well, away home with you until the good Lord decides.

FIRST CHILD. Is he dying then?

SECOND CHILD. Will he go to Jesus?

SISTER. Are you looking for a crack from the ruler? Silent as bones, I think I said. Go home, Mary. Go home and stay there. What your mother is about to let you come . . .

MARY. She's taken up with the baby, Sister.

SISTER. Taken up or no, she's no right . . . Run away now, this instant. We'll pray for the little one. Don't stop, Mary, don't dawdle or pass a word upon the way, run. (*Calling.*) And when you get there, close the door, and don't open it to a living soul save the doctor. (*Quietly.*) And the fever cart.

CHILDREN (*Whispering*). The fever cart. Fever. Fever, fever, fever, fever. (*Held under first few lines.*)

MARY (*over*). I ran then, sliding down the hill over the wet reek of turf, away from them all. And they sent the fever cart to us, and they took our Michael away. It was dark in the cart, all wood, with a little slit of a window high up and a wooden shelf on either side. I laid him on a shelf. I wrapped him in my shawl and laid him there. But when I tried to get in with him, to hold him, so he'd have the feel of me with him — he was only a little bit of a babe, his life hadn't got far on, and he was all the toys I had, and it was dark in the cart, dark — when I climbed in they flung me to the cobble-stones and my mother held me down. And all my screams and all my struggling and all my hate didn't stop the bolt across the wooden door, the driver's whip, the horse's hooves, the neighbours' peering through the window cracks, the rain. I stayed there on the cobbles while they rattled him out of my life and into the next world. My mother held me down. She did that. She did that to me.

The sound of a church bell. Wind. A horsecart goes by. A church.

MARY. I hate this place, Father John, and everyone in it. When I'm grown up I'm going to kill them all.

FATHER JOHN. That's your sorrow speaking child. Life is hard. There's not a family round here that hasn't dwindled in numbers, you've only to look about. We're only lent to one another. Poor little babe. His soul has fled to sacred realms above.

MARY. Will we meet there? Will he know me do you think, Father? All those babies up in Heaven, will I forget which one he is?

FATHER JOHN. Of course we'll know our loved ones, and they will know us. Why don't you read your Prayer Book, Mary? What does it matter what sort of hard, drudging life we live down here, that's only like the husk that hides the grain of corn. When we have our grand new resurrection bodies we shall feel more ready to meet our long lost dear ones. Do you understand?

MARY. Yes, Father. No. No, I don't.

(*Over.*) Another baby died, and another, without a name between them, poor weak articles. My father drank his work away, some nights he'd beat us for an hour for a bit of cheer, I've the marks of the buckle still. But I read books I stole from school by candlelight, I saw a circus with spangled girls and a tatooed man who swallowed swords and fire. A boy called Seamus carved me a box with a fitted lit in exchange for a squint beneath my shift behind the giant burdock leaves. There was more to life than the crack of my father's belt, there was a world out there. I grew. I looked older than I was. I took over the cockle stall, alongside the soap and candle sellers. I hid what money I could in the carved box. One night of rain and beer and tears my mother screamed and screamed. I ran through the dark for the doctor, and he came in his trap and he took her away. My father sobbed. She wanted me, she stretched out her hand for me, but the doctor ordered me to stay. They were going to open her up, he said, and take the baby from her. I knew they'd kill her. Just like Michael. I saw in my mind a fearful thing — her white face, the slow rip across her stomach and the baby falling out from her entrails, falling. Well, she did die. Next night. And there was just my father and me and that was that.

A churchyard. 1888. MARY is sixteen. Sound of passing bell again, lonely wind, a bird is singing nearby.

MARY. I'm leaving Father, I've enough saved for my passage, there's nothing to keep me now. I don't give a rat in hell for anybody here. I'm going across the water. I'm going to the United States of America.

FATHER JOHN. Think, Mary. It might go hard with you. God knows when we'd see you again.

MARY. Perhaps never, and none the worse for that. Oh, Father, have you not listened to the men down by the Customs House? I have. It's like Paradise they say. We don't live no better than dogs here.

FATHER JOHN. Thou shalt be mine in the days when I make up my jewels, saith the Lord.

MARY. I can't wait for that. I'm going to be someone *now*.

FATHER JOHN. Well, well, well. Little Molly Malone. My blessings go with you. Nothing will do but a place in the history books, is that it?

MARY. Yes. That's it.

A long blast on a ship's hooter — mix into cries and shouts. Chains rattling as a crowded ship lands. A band plays 'Washington Post'.

VOICE ONE. Here at the sea-washed, sunset gates shall stand a mighty woman with a torch . . .

VOICE TWO. . . . the scum of creation has been dumped on us. The most dangerous and corrupting hordes of the Old World have invaded us . . .

MARY. It's Paradise. A city of towers, mountains made of brick. And sunshine. Hot meat every day, and work, and beds as wide as

Sackville Street, and everyone a pair of boots . . .

VOICE ONE. Give me your tired, your poor, your huddled masses yearning to breathe free . . .

VOICE TWO. . . . the vice and crime which they have planted in our midst are sickening and terrifying . . .

MARY. I'll have a house, with a porch and a rocking chair. Across the water I can be someone, I know it. There's nothing'll stop me. I'm strong. I'll work and work. I'm going to amount to something.

(*Shouts. Chains. Hooters.*)

VOICE ONE. Send the homeless, tempest-tossed to me. I lift my lamp beside the golden door.

Immigration shed. Thump of rubber stamp.

OFFICIAL. Welcome to the land of opportunity. I wish you good fortune in your new life. OK. Joseph Platski. Tailor. Next! Name?

MARY. Mary Malone, sir.

OFFICIAL. Where's your label? Get that shawl off . . . clutching all that stuff . . . lean nearer. Mary Mallon.

MARY. No. Malone. That's Mallon you've writ there. M. . .A. . .L. . .O. .

OFFICIAL. You insolent?

MARY. No, sir.

OFFICIAL. Looking for another sea voyage?

MARY. Oh God no sir.

OFFICIAL. Then that's your name, sister. Got any other thoughts? OK. Now the medical. General health? You look in good shape. Got a glass eye, Mary Mallon, cork leg?

MARY. I have not.

OFFICIAL. No glass eyes. No cork legs. Infectious diseases. Smallpox, scarlet fever, diptheria, typhoid, tuberculosis, etc. etc?

MARY. No sir.

OFFICIAL. No infectious diseases. Weak heart?

MARY. No.

OFFICIAL. No. The crossing weeds them out. Deaf, no, dumb, no, blind, no. Epilepsy? Incontinence?

MARY. If they come out in spots, sir, no. I'm always well.

OFFICIAL. I'll put you down for no. You a prostitute?

MARY. God save us, no.

OFFICIAL. OK. That's the medical. (*Thump of stamp.*) Type of employment. Any special skills? Academic qualifications? Secretarial, nursing, teaching, manual etc. etc?

MARY. Well. I had the cockle barrow. Whelks, mussels . . .

OFFICIAL. Fish. Food. You can cook. They need cooks. That's fine. You're in.

MARY. But sir, I . . .

OFFICIAL. Sister, beat it. I got no time. Look behind you. Thousands jostling to take your place. I got no time. Welcome to the land of opportunity, I wish you good fortune in your new life. OK Mary Mallon. (*Thump.*) Cook. (*Thump.*) Next!

Music. Cut to 'Stars and Stripes Forever'. Hold beneath first lines of speech.

MARY (*voice over*). I threw my label, Mary Malone, female, Irish, unemployed, into the brown river. It didn't float for long. It was Mary Mallon, American citizen, cook, who passed through the golden door and into the city. The rattle and the clatter, and the dirty breathless wonder of it. I found a fortune card on a bench. 'You are destined for great things' it said, 'you have a lucky hand.' I got a job in an eating house on the West Side — I shared a room and a bed with Agnes, a laundress, and her child. I cooked corned beef and cabbage, sausages and hash for fourteen hours a day. Life was grand, I'd done right to cross the water, I had leather shoes, Agnes and Elspeth were my sisters, I put money by. I bought Agnes a lace collar and stockings with lace tops, Elspeth a hoop and a pair of red boots. I bought myself a book.

A tenement room. Night. The distant sound of a cat.

AGNES. You'll spoil your eyes, Mary.

MARY. I've got to study this. I'm not cooking cabbage for ever. Page thirty four, peach pickle. Doesn't that make the juices spring into your mouth?

AGNES. If it was me I'd learn as I went along and get some sleep.

MARY. The chef's a stick, Agnes. He can just about peel a potato. I'll teach myself, thank you.

AGNES. Look at Elspeth. Hugging them boots to her as if they was a doll. I can't get them off her.

ELSPETH. I'm hungry.

AGNES. Elspeth! I thought you were asleep.

ELSPETH. I was. It's hot. I'm hungry.

MARY. Blanch the almonds — what does blanch mean, do you think.

Oh, bless us and save us I almost forgot. Reach under the bed, Elspeth, there's a basin there. No, not the chamber. A basin. Covered with a cloth.

ELSPETH. This?

MARY. Hand it over. Now. Sit up, everyone. Houpla!

ELSPETH. Gee willikins.

MARY. Trifle.

ELSPETH. Where'd it come from?

MARY. I made it. Filched the stuff from the kitchens, bit by bit.

AGNES. Mary. What a fool thing to do.

MARY; I've got to learn somehow. They won't miss it. Anyway, I'll be moving on soon. Eat it up and shame the devil. We'll have to pass the spoon round.

AGNES. It's good, Mary.

MARY. Could be worse. Too much egg.

ELSPETH. Will you fix us something good to eat every night, Mary? Will you? Filch it? Will you?

MARY. You eat like that every night, you'll soon have a belly like a bean pot.

ELSPETH. Will you, though? Something real cold?

MARY. Maybe.

ELSPETH. I'm mighty glad you're here with us, Mary. Don't move on. It's good with you around.

MARY. Blatherer. Eat up and go to sleep.

MARY (*voice over*). I did move on. I had to. The typhoid got them. The doctor hung carbolic sheets around the room. Rats scuttled out through the sulphur fumes. I burned a lot of things. I nursed them both. Didn't do much good. Agnes screamed 'Don't let them take me to the pest house, Mary'; and Elspeth — 'Help me Mary' she whispered, 'my belly's killing me.' What can you do? I haven't bothered with caring for people again, it isn't worth it.(*Street noises. Horse drawn traffic.*) I walked about, and ate, and worked, and got myself through the days. (*Train hooter.*) And more days. I moved from chilli and hash up to pigeon pie and flummery tipsy cake and up from there to larded capon, bechamel sauce and lemon chiffon pie. Hotels and private houses. (*Accordian: Molly Malone.*) There was a lot of typhoid about in those days, you've to expect it, like there'll be a bad egg in a bowl now and then — but I didn't stop to let it catch me, there's no use tempting Fate. I bettered myself. One day the agency sent me to a summer residence, a great white wandering place with marble floors and a fountain in the hall.

A rich country summer residence.

MRS PALMER. 'She did well enough. She had her repertoire, and we got to know that repertoire tolerably well, but she was eager enough to learn.' Good. So many servants nowadays are very much alive to the dread of anything in the shape of a task. Are you strong?

MARY. Yes, madam.

MRS PALMER. Good again. Frailty is *not* a quality I admire. Are you a believer?

MARY. Yes, madam.

MRS PALMER. The servants are left to spend their Sundays pretty much as they choose, apart from appearances at morning and evening service. I hope you will pray for reliability. That *is* a quality I admire. They come and go so, servants now. So many transients. I hope you're here to stay. The Irish are notoriously unreliable.

MARY. Oh, madam, I am. And I'm not Irish, I'm an American citizen, I've the papers to prove it . . .

MRS PALMER. Yes. Well. We shall see what we shall see. Now. Terms. You will have a girl under you and forty-five dollars a month. We are simple folk — to us the word extravagant is synonymous with the word barbaric. If great granmama could rough it so may we. That door leads to your sitting room. Breakfast — five courses will suffice — shirred eggs, broiled fish, steak, you know the sort of thing; light luncheon — picnics, clambakes, no flimflammery. Please attend to your nails, grime is an abomination to Mr. Palmer, and contain your hair. Ah hah. Our latest scientific marvel . . . our ice box.

She opens the fridge door. From time to time during MRS PALMER's *speech* MARY *murmers assent etc. as she follows her.*

MARY (*over*). Yes, madam, no, madam, three bags full, madam, oh Mary Mallon, you've arrived. Forty-seven rooms, and this is just the summer place. Women and children all in white under the elms on the edge of the lake, and gardeners tying roses, sweeping paths. Fanlights, pillars, fancy pompadoodles on the ceiling, think of all those mats shook out of all those windows of a morning. In my room there's rugs on top of carpets. I'm somebody. I've done it, Father John. Taties and rats for breakfast, eh? Oh no, not now. Can you hear me, Joseph O'Malley and Mary Trundle and all the Lynch boys? Can you hear me, you poor, lost, faded articles. It's Molly Malone, stinks like a fish, calling across the water. You've babies of your own now, squalling, grabbing for bits of bread. For me, five courses will suffice. No flimflammery. My hair contained. Oh Lord above, I think I'll stay for ever. The card was right. I have a lucky hand. Now. The latest scientific marvel, she said. 'A miracle box' it says here . . . 'way in advance of any other make . . . at long last it is possible to store your perishables in perfect safety.'

A midsummer picnic. 'In the Good Old Summertime' on the phonograph. Evening birdsong. Languid chatter. What we hear is at one end of a long table.

MRS PALMER I have sat in the sun too long today. My nose is positively pink. Aunt Lettie, there is a petal about to land upon the mayonnaise.

FRANKLYN. It's too stupid for words to do anything else in life but simply be here, stuffing oneself lasciviously with spiced oysters en plein air.

LANCE. Where is Morgan? Still on the wire to Boston or Philadelphia or whatever? Eternally toiling?

MRS PALMER. Poor Morgan. I trust he will join us shortly. To tell the truth, he is unwell.

LANCE. How tiresome for him. Is it serious?

MRS PALMER. No, no. Trifling. A headache. Vague discomforts.

TUTOR. I hope Mr Palmer will soon be recovered.

FRANKLYN. Oh, those lobsters, standing there for all the world like the three wise men in a boat. Lavinia, with hand on heart I declare you the perfect hostess.

MRS PALMER. Thank you, Franklyn. Ah. Dessert. From our icebox, our latest toy. Put it there.

All admire the icecream. Laughter. Clapping.

FRANKLYN. Silence. I insist upon silence.

MRS PALMER. Aunt Lettie, waft away that moth for heavens' sake.

FRANKLYN. We have here a confection before which one should bow, solemnly and profoundly, as though performing an act of worship.

LANCE. Do you know to whom we are indebted for the introduction of ice cream?

FRANKLYN. Presumably Lavinia's excellent cook.

LANCE. No. Not that good soul. Catherina de Medici. Now, who dares a slice?

Ad lib laughter. Through it . . .

TUTOR. Mrs. Palmer, I wonder if I might be forgiven. I feel a trifle out of sorts, in fact more than a trifle. In fact . . .

MRS PALMER. Heavens. How white you are. I trust it is nothing sinister.

FRANKLYN. Lance, you have mortally terrified the tutor.

TUTOR. It is not sudden, all day I . . .

MRS PALMER. By all means leave us. Aunt Lettie, there is a beetle marching straight for the butter. Go. Rest a little.

TUTOR. I can't see . . . my nose is bleeding. I . . . excuse me, I . . .

He crashes into the table. Consternation. Glass and china splinter.

Cut to patient's steady breathing.

A bedroom. This scene at great speed. A long moan from the PATIENT.

NURSE. Temperature ninety nine degrees.

FIRST DOCTOR. The patient presents us with the following symptoms. Slight dry cough —

SECOND DOCTOR. Dull and continuous headache.

THIRD DOCTOR. A certain abdominal discomfort —

ALL. In my considered opinion we have here —

FIRST DOCTOR. Tonsilitis.

SECOND DOCTOR. Bronchitis.

THIRD DOCTOR. Gastro-enteritis.

FIRST DOCTOR. Plenty of rest, plenty of fresh air.

SECOND DOCTOR. A spoonful of this thrice daily.

THIRD DOCTOR. A couple of these twice nightly.

ALL. There's a great deal of this around.

MARY (*over*). Invalid jelly. What ails them I wonder. 'Twelve shanks of mutton, scrub and soak.' I could do with a sip myself, I feel like holy hell. It's that dream. I can't get out from under it. (*Fade in children's whispers.*) 'A faggot of sweet herbs.' It was here, in the kitchen. I heard a sort of rustle, and I looked up, and saw cocoons stuck to the ceiling big as water melons. I could see clear through them, and inside was moths, big and black like crows, oh, I can feel the flap of them now. 'Three quarts of water.' What's my skimmer doing in the candle box? They had mouths like people's mouths, and they whispered, rustling, over and over, (*Fever whispers.*) 'misbegotten Mary, misbegotten Mary.' What kind of a word is that? Misbegotten. Mace, mace, three blades of mace. It's not a word I ever think of. Ah, the hell with it. I was put on this earth to nourish folk, and that's what I do.

ALL (*round*). In my considered opinion we have here —

FIRST DOCTOR. Influenza.

SECOND DOCTOR. Salmonella.

THIRD DOCTOR. Lobar pneumonia.

FIRST DOCTOR. You're doing fine.

SECOND DOCTOR. Keep up the good work.

THIRD DOCTOR. Double the dosage.

ALL. Soon have you up and about.

NURSE. Temperature one hundred and four degrees.

Heavy fevered breathing.

FIRST DOCTOR. We are confronted now with a new and alarming set of symptoms. This dullness and delirium —

SECOND DOCTOR. This crop of rose spots erupting on the chest —

THIRD DOCTOR. This dusty, damp, hay-like smell, once experienced, never forgotten —

ALL (*round*). In our considered opinion we have here . . .

PATIENT (*a terrifying whisper*). TYPHOID.

MARY (*over*). Oh, God, it's happened again. Oh, God in Heaven, why? I want to stay here. I'm tired of moving on. This is my home. But it's no good. I know what ails them now. All that clanging palaver of slop pails. Sheets across the doors. Commotion. The stench of liquid chlorine of lime upon the floor, infectious vapours everywhere. Eight of them sick, the (*Whispers.*) children too. Why children? There's no sense to the world. Make us some barley sugar, cookie dear, they said, and now . . . The fever won't catch me, days and weeks in a raging delirium, I've seen what it can do. It pays to be stubborn in this old life. Oh, God, look at the sun on the lake, why here? Well, we must do what we must do.

The summer residence

MAID. There's a scientific gentleman, ma'am, come about the water.

SOPER. My assistant, Elliot Kendall. I am Dr Soper.

MRS PALMER. Dear me, more investigations. We have been investigated so many times . . .

SOPER. A mysterious case, ma'am. One that has baffled many good men. I am intrigued.

MRS PALMER. Well. This is the room that they have all made use of. I have ordered the windows to be left open — my doctors assure me the enemies of typhoid are cleanliness, sobriety and judicious ventilation.

KENDALL. And Dr Soper.

MRS PALMER. I beg your pardon?

KENDALL. Enemy of typhoid. Dr Soper.

MRS PALMER. I hope so. I hope so indeed. Oh dear, I'm sure we have always led clean and sober lives — I cannot imagine why we have been so singled out. Well, we may at least be grateful that my children are recovered. Dr Soper, are not all these files sufficiently bulging? Some of us are far from well. Could we not be spared further interrogation?

SOPER. The questions are not trifling. We have to pinpoint the mode of transmission, ma'am. Track it to its source.

MRS PALMER. It's all so wearisome.

SOPER. Less wearisome, I think, than looking for another home. If we fail to find the source of contamination I shall be forced to burn this house, ma'am.

MRS PALMER. Burn it?

SOPER. To the ground.

MRS PALMER. That is a monstrous threat — the carvings, they're priceless, irreplaceable.

SOPER. Fever is remorseless, ma'am. We have to fight it.

MRS PALMER. Look at my ceilings. They're Italian.

SOPER. Boil. Bury. Burn. I have done it before, and will again.

KENDALL. Dr Soper is not known as the Epidemic Fighter for nothing.

SOPER. But we shall dig out the answer here, I'm sure of it. Given co-operation.

MRS PALMER. Naturally, Dr Soper, Mr Kendall, you may count upon us. Should you require anything, anything at all, please ring this bell. Although I must confess I am not at all sure who will answer. We are sadly depleted. I often felt how pleasant it would be not to have all that fuss with servants underfoot, but now . . . At any rate, you may ring the bell and hope.

She fades out of the door. KENDALL *closes it.*

SOPER. Silly woman.

KENDALL. Was that true? About the burning?

SOPER. Once. My first case. Magnificent house. Totally contaminated.

KENDALL. And you razed it to the ground?

SOPER. Had to. I was a young whippersnapper. The family were not well pleased. Hand me the records, would you.

KENDALL. It's certainly palatial. I'll wager the sewers are fed by gold pipes.

SOPER. Many a palace is a pig pen in its hidden recesses. Still. A change from the Lower East Side outbreaks. Now. Water. Always start with water, Kendall. Here you are. Who's the analyst?

KENDALL. Dr Tapper.

SOPER. First class. I know his work. A careful man. Right. Faucet in house?

KENDALL. Sanitarily pure.

SOPER. Outside tank?

KENDALL. Safe.

SOPER. Pump over well?

KENDALL. No evidence of pollution.

SOPER. Inside tank?

KENDALL. Typhoid from this source impossible.

SOPER. Cesspools?

KENDALL. Cleaned in April. Clear.

SOPER. Privies used by the servants?

KENDALL. Ditto.

SOPER. Inadequate infiltration?

KENDALL. No.

SOPER. Building on gathering ground?

KENDALL. No.

SOPER. Surface contamination of shallow wells?

KENDALL. No.

SOPER. Damn.

KENDALL. I think we may rationally assume, sir, that it is not the water.

SOPER. Oh, do you? I want fluorescin tests in the following places — bowl of water closet, cesspool, stable manure vault, privy, and ditto on the adjacent property.

KENDALL. You said Dr Tapper was a first class man.

SOPER. The best.

KENDALL. Then why, when his report conclusively proves . . .

SOPER. When you work with me, Kendall, you will never take half measures. You will never be slipshod. Never take anything for granted.

KENDALL. No sir.

SOPER. Nature exposes, man diagnoses. And we are responsible for people's loves.

KENDALL. Sir.

SOPER. Be cussed, Kendall. Be cussed as the very devil.

Piano version of Sweet Molly Malone.

MARY (*over*). Mayonnaise of salmon, ribs of lamb, tongue, collared eel, raised pie, lark pie, lobster, baked spice ham and every kind of feathered edible, all for one course on one day for a summer's entertainment. A long, long way from torn sheets cracking out over a wet hillside, and a bit of a pig at the back, and hauling that stinking barrow down streets just about wide enough for two sparrows to walk abreast. A lot of world between me and poor Molly, with bread and sugar every mortal dinner of her life, and her hands red raw with the cold of them cockles and mussels.

Fade.

Summer residence

KENDALL. Would you care for a graham cracker, sir? I think I'll have one. Unless of course we're going to stop for luncheon.

SOPER. It has to come from somewhere. Remind me, when was the first person taken sick.

KENDALL. Mr Weedon Palmer. August twenty-third.

SOPER. And the last?

KENDALL. The gardener. September third.

SOPER. Two weeks.

KENDALL. All the reports suggest contagion from Mr Palmer.

SOPER. I discard that. The sicknesses are staggered because incubation varies with the individual. They all contracted it at the same time, I'm sure of it. In any case, it doesn't matter a rap who infected whom. How did the *first* one occur, that's what's crucial.

KENDALL. Should we discuss it at luncheon, sir? Only it is a quarter after four. We made no stop yesterday, nor the day before. Mrs Soper said to remind you.

SOPER. Mrs Soper is a thoroughly good woman. But she has no grasp of epidemiology. If you wish to stuff yourself with food all day, that's your affair.

KENDALL. No sir. Just a cracker now and then.

SOPER. Kendall, we're faced with an isolated cluster of cases. No one who has had typhoid has lived in this house or visited during the whole summer. Milk, cream, fruit and vegetables are supplied by local sources — no other household in Oyster Bay buying from the same source has succumbed. We have eliminated flies and water. What have we missed. Some peculiar event, perhaps, on or before August twentieth. Clambake, hayride, picnic, church, tennis party, some such gathering. Are these people hiding something, perhaps without knowing? There's an answer somewhere. Why hasn't someone visited the family from outside — I need an outsider, dammit. What's the secret in here, what in hell have I missed? It HAS to come from somewhere.

MARY (*over*). When I have children of my own, I shall say to them — Come now children, never stand to eat, the food goes down to your feet. A kitchen's like a temple — I want a holy hush when I take off the lid. Now. Fold your hands. Thank God for something in the pot.
Good food
good meat
good Lord
let's eat.

Summer residence.

SOPER. For God's sake, man, be careful with that sample. Oh, Lord, the indolence. The inertia.

KENDALL. You're cracking your knuckles, sir. Dr Soper you look terrible. Your face is grey.

SOPER. I'm going mad through getting nowhere. It's nothing. A cold.

KENDALL. Are you sure? You should take care of yourself, eat regularly.
SOPER. Don't *you* mother me, I have enough from Mrs Soper. Look, every time I get a sore throat or a belly ache I think it's my turn now. Do you understand? It's nothing. It'll pass. It's a cold.

KENDALL. I'm really pleasured that you feel that way sir too. I worry about dust all the time. I breathe as lightly as I can. I have the feeling there's just one baccillus, lurking there in the dust, a soldier's bullet, with my name on.

SOPER. Forget it. Get absorbed. Dig deeper, ferret. Get absorbed.

On slight echo.

FIRST CHILD. Cook has snaffled us some of the pudding. I told her us poor fellows are starved.

SECOND CHILD. Isn't it a beauty.

FIRST CHILD. Harry. I'm sure we don't have to fall upon it like starving wolves. I'll share it out.

SECOND CHILD. Layer upon layer. Yum.

FIRST CHILD. That's not a fair share.

SECOND CHILD. It is too.

FIRST CHILD. It is not. You've the largest piece yourself.

SECOND CHILD. I have not.

FIRST CHILD. You have so.

Fade on their quarrelling.

Summer Residence.

KENDALL. That was a fine cake, Effie. Could you rustle up some more, do you think? I'm truly hungry.

MAID. I surely could, sir. That was Mary's special, that was.

KENDALL. My compliments to Mary. Please convey them.

MAID. Oh, she's gone, sir, but she left the recipe.

SOPER. Left? Who left?

MAID. Mary, sir. The last cook, sir. But like I bin saying she's gone, sir.

SOPER. When?

MAID. Since last month, sir.

SOPER. When? When last month?

MAID. 'Bout when the fever came, sir. Well, just after. I recall the day 'cause I was setting the tea leaves by for shaking on the rugs, pails and pails we had . . .

SOPER. Where did she go, dammit?

MAID. Don't know sir. One day there she wasn't. Upped and gone. Heavens to Betsy, why do you look that way, sir. Did I do wrong to tell?

Spoons tap out Sweet Molly Malone.

MRS PALMER. Mary Mallon? Yes, she was a servant here.

SOPER. What was she like? Describe her.

MRS PALMER. Oh, gracious. I hardly noticed. A handsome, healthy, large girl, large hands, large eyes. Only tolerably clean, but one must make allowances for transients I suppose.

SOPER. She was an immigrant?

MRS PALMER. Irish. You may safely rely upon their unreliability I fear.

SOPER. It was monumentally unreliable not to speak of her before. Where is she now?

MRS PALMER. I assume gone off with some fancy man.

SOPER. I have no use for assumptions. This is urgent. Where might she be?

MRS PALMER. Heavens, Dr Soper, ask a servant. If you can find one in this decimated household. Bulletins of distress seem to reach me almost hourly. That class of person is ungrateful and that's all there is to be said. Forty-five dollars a month! They hold us to ransom. The domestic problem is with us always. Dr Soper, there seems no path but downard on that score.

Humming and spoons.

SOPER. My outsider. It could be. It could just be.

KENDALL. Dr Soper. Please don't crack your knuckles.

SOPER. Koch.

KENDALL. I beg your pardon?

SOPER. Robert Koch. The greatest bacteriologist alive. Typhusbazillen-trägerin. Strassberg. The carrier principle, 1903.

KENDALL. Dr Soper, I'm lost.

SOPER. You should read more, Kendall, keep up to date. Germany has always been ahead of the New World in the study of medicine. Man may be the cause of the continuance of the disease. What do you say to that?

KENDALL. I'm still lost, sir.

SOPER. We know the disease is spread by contagion, through the reproduction of a specific organism within the living body and through the excretion of this infective material in the faeces and urine — we know all that. Now, Koch was called to a bakery in Strassberg where there had been repeated outbreaks. Mystification. The bakeshop was clean, the water pure. Koch found there was a human carrier, not flies, not dust, human — the woman who ran the shop. Do not interrupt, uninformed interruptions are an anathema. She had had typhoid years before and had apparently fully recovered. Mark that word apparently. She appeared harmless. She was able to go about her business like an ordinary, healthy person. But — a monumental but — her body still excreted germs.

KENDALL. So the fever was passed on . . .

SOPER. And on, and on. By the hands of those who prepare food. I think we might accept this Mallon woman, strong, healthy, transient and only tolerably clean, could have . . . a peculiar event on or around August twentieth.

KENDALL. Where are we, August twenty-three, twenty-two, twenty-one, twenty. Um. There was a picnic . . .

SOPER. Did they all attend?

KENDALL. I think so, yes.

SOPER. Did they or did they not?

KENDALL. Yes sir. They did.

SOPER. We must divide. You're good at ingratiating yourself with the ladies — I'll take the others. Ask them what they ate. Never mind the cooked stuff, it's the raw food we're after. Watercress, oysters, clams, salad, mayonnaise, icecream, you know the sort of thing. Give them time. Make sure the sick are not too upset to think. Don't alarm them.

KENDALL. Right.

SOPER. And Kendall. Memory is a strange and cloudy thing. Help them. Persist. But don't insist.

KENDALL. No sir.

SOPER. But do persist.

KENDALL. Yes sir.

SOPER. My God. My neck is prickling.

Sound of humming and spoons.

SOPER. Now that I know I feel curiously empty. There it is. Ice cream with fresh peaches cut up and frozen in it. Beautifully lethal. I suppose no better way could be found for a cook to cleanse her hands of microbes and infect a family.

KENDALL. Of course we still don't know this Mary Mallon has had typhoid.

SOPER. No. She's not perfect, but she's all we've got. Where is she? Where is she? We must go hunting, Kendall. Weeks of rattling across the land in trains and trolleys, months of miasma and evasions and suspicion and slammed doors.

KENDALL. It looks to be a very dreary autumn, sir.

SOPER. You'll love it. The very thought sends my adrenalin rushing.

KENDALL. Poor Mrs Soper. So set upon your joining her in Atlanta.

SOPER. Nothing to be done. Mary Mallon must be found.

KENDALL. I guess she's dangerous?

SOPER. Dangerous? The woman is a walking pestilence.

A Drawing room. New York. Music — Ragtime — traffic etc.

LADY. I am not interested in references, Mary. I prefer to rely upon my own judgement. Our last cook was with us many happy years until her marriage. Why did you leave your last employment, Mary?

MARY. Sickness, madam.

LADY. Oh. Theirs or yours?

MARY. Theirs.

LADY. Ah. And the situation before that?

MARY. The same reason, madam.

LADY. Sickness again?

MARY. Yes, madam.

LADY. Yours?

MARY. Theirs.

LADY. We must trust we are of hardier stock, must we not? I think you'll suit. I think you'll suit very well.

Sound of trains.

WOMAN. Mrs Goodge's Employment Agency.

WOMAN. Mrs Stricker's Domestics.

KENDALL. Excuse me, ma'am. I'm doing an employment verification on a Miss Mary Mallon.

WOMAN. Mary Mallon?

WOMAN. She came to us highly recommended and left of her own accord.

WOMAN. There was a note, as I recall, pinned to the bolster . . .

WOMAN. She left some articles behind . . . trifles — a hair brush, a cheap clasp . . .

MARY. Steamer, skewers, dripping pan and stand, pair of bellows, jelly moulds, meat screen . . .

SOPER. How long was she with you?

KENDALL. Do you know where she went?

MAN. You from the relief?

MAN. Who wants to know?

SOPER. The victims who succumbed, in chronological order.
Maramoneck 1900 —
the daughter of the head of the family, two maid servants, one coloured, the wife of the head of the family, the daughter of a tenant, a gardener.
Dark Harbour, Maine 1901 —
a laundress, a coloured chauffeur, the son of a tenant . . .

KENDALL. Does anyone know this woman?

SOPER. Mary Mallon.

SEVERAL. Mary Mallon?

WOMAN. I'm afraid not.

MAN. Sorry no.

WOMAN. You've got me beat there.

MAN. Don't know nothing about nothing. Never heard of no one.

MARY. The common black draught. Infuse half an ounce of Alexandrian senna, three ounces of Epsom salts, two drachms of bruised ginger and coriander seeds in equal parts for several hours in a pint of boiling water, strain the liquor and add two drams of spirits of the whole. That should put them back on their feet in no time . . .

SOPER. It's clear she was responsible for the following outbreaks, in chronological order — Maramoneck 1900, New York 1901, Dark Harbour, Maine, 1901, Sands Point, Long Island, 1904, Tuxedo, New York, 1906, Oyster Bay, 1906 and now —

An office. Bang straight in.

SOPER. New York, 1907. I've found her. Kendall. I got a lead. I've found her. In a brownstone. An old fashioned stoop house on Park Avenue.

KENDALL. Good God. At last. Has she infected anyone?

SOPER. Of course. A laundress. And a child. A little girl of ten.

KENDALL. But you've found her. Dr Soper, you're amazing. This calls for a celebration, a drink of something. We should go somewhere plush. Why are you so flat about it, sir? Has she had typhoid? Were the tests positive? Too soon to say, I guess. Have a cigar, sir, a drink, something. What happened?

SOPER. I opened the kitchen door, and there she was.

KENDALL. Don't stop. What did she look like?

SOPER. A woman, cooking.

KENDALL. Was she like the descriptions? All those files, I feel I'd know her anywhere. They're in my heart, like Calais.

SOPER. She looked like any woman in a kitchen, like I remember my mother — hot skin, sleeves rolled up, blowing a strand of hair out of her eyes. She was frowning into a saucepan. She held the lid in one hand, and drips sizzled onto the stove. Then she clamped the lid down, turned to the table, picked up a cleaver, and tested the blade against her thumb. Those hands, Kendall. All these months of tracking, and there were those hands. That sharp cleaver against her thumb. I shan't forget.

KENDALL. But what happened? What did you say?

SOPER. She thought I was the ice man, but not for long. What *do* you say, Kendall? I showed her my list of where she'd worked and how in every single house people had been sick or died. I asked her if she did not think it strange that fever seemed to follow her. I told her how fever could be passed from one person to another, I used simple terms a child could understand. I told her no-one blamed her, it was an act of God. What do you say, Kendall? How in God's name do you tell a person you suspect them of making people sick?

Kitchen. Sizzlings. Bubblings. A great burst of laughter.

MARY. You're never a true medical man. You've come to sell tonics or powders or some such. Testimonies of miracles a saint wouldn't be ashamed of at fifty cents a box. Well. There's the door.

SOPER. Miss Mallon. I am an epidemiologist of international repute. I also represent the Health Department.

MARY. Aren't you the eighth wonder of the world then. How did the germs get in me, tell me that, leave alone get out again?

SOPER. I think you once had the disease yourself.

MARY. Wrong. I never have.

SOPER. Possibly so lightly you were unaware of it.

MARY. Never. I have no time to be sick, and that's that.

SOPER. Did someone in your family suffer — parent, brother, sister, someone?

MARY. Move. Move out of my way. If this stock clouds over I have to start from scratch.

He follows her as she stamps and clangs her way round the kitchen working.

SOPER. The germs have stayed in your gall bladder, breeding and multiplying . . .

MARY. You think I choose who lives and who dies? Very flattering, but that's God's work. You're a quack or a crank or something, be accusing me of witchcraft next.

SOPER. It is to do with your hands. When you go to the toilet the germs are carried afterwards onto the food that you prepare and the people who eat this food get sick. If you would wash your hands more often . . .

MARY. You have the gall to say I'm dirty? Look at my hands. Can you see any germs on them? Of course not. that's not germs there, that's freckles. Specks of ink here, from writing lists. See, I can't lick them away, that's ink. Scars. Hot fat, knives, work scars, can't lick them away, life isn't soft down here. But they're clean hands like anybody else's, as clean as yours, be sure of that, Mister Doctor from the Health Department. Ah, well, this here in my nails is flour, but I can soon pick that out, that's not germs.

SOPER. My dear woman, you can't *see* germs.

MARY. No you can not.

SOPER. I could show you billions. Under a microscope. Come with me to the Research Laboratory. You can answer a few simple questions, we'll make some tests, take some samples of your blood and urine and faeces, and in return I'll show you what germs truly look like. Is that a bargain?

MARY. If it's dirt you're looking for you want to be next door but one, the cook there has fingernails the colour of mushrooms. That's it.

They'll have sent you to the wrong place, these brownstones look all alike.

SOPER. There's no mistake, Miss Mallon.

MARY. Corner of Park and Sixtieth. She's the one you want.

SOPER. Come to the Laboratory. I'll prove it to you.

MARY. On the corner. Turn left. I'll tell you something else — I may as well be helpful — she'll scoop all the mess on the plates, fishskin, mustard, pips, gristle, all of it into her stockpot and call it soup. There'll be billions of germs swimming around — you can have a fine day of it putting your microscope on to that lot. Now I've done what I can for you, and I'll ask you to go.

SOPER. Look, nothing bad's going to happen to you, there's no call to cry.

MARY. Don't flatter yourself, that's not tears, that's onions. Take more than a mouthful of twaddle to break me. Now will you move OUT of my way or as God is my judge I'll call the police to you for all the Health Department's supposed to come into it.

She sharpens the cleaver on a steel.

SOPER. I'll go if you come with me. A few specimens, and then you may go home. I have a cab waiting. Trust me. Come with me.

MARY. Trust you? Go with you? A man who says I'm dirty? I kill people?

SOPER. I give you my solemn word no harm will come to you. The Research Laboratory is just like a hospital . . .

MARY. A hospital? Oh God, are you sent to murder me.

SOPER. Murder you? Balderdash. All I'm asking for is specimens, some tests, some samples . . .

MARY. I know what happens in hospitals. When doctors get to you. They bolt the doors. Like mother. Like Michael. They bolt the doors and they drive you away and they put the knife on you and rip you open. And you don't come back. I'll not let you take me. I'll carve you first.

SOPER. Put that down. Goddammit, woman, haven't you heard a word I've said . . .

MARY (*advancing with the knife*). It won't be me that's murdered. I'll slice every inch of meat from your bones, I'll fillet you. Get out of here. Get out, get out, get OUT.

An office.

SOPER. Picture it, Kendall. The knife blade gleamed, soups boiled and bubbled furiously. A hundred and sixty pounds of enraged womanhood, in her healthy prime, eyes blasting, sprang on me. I somehow stumbled to the door, she heaved the cleaver at me, I fell up the stairs, took to my heels and fled followed by great metal lids and a full ashcan. I left my hat and stick behind, my favourite stick.

KENDALL. Good God. You were lucky to escape. She must be mad.

SOPER. No. I think not mad. In some way fighting for her life.

KENDALL. At any rate, you're safe. Now it's a matter for the police.

SOPER. Fiddlesticks. She's my responsibility. I'm not about to lose her now. I returned, with dread I may say, twice in the next two days. I absolutely failed. There was nothing for it but to follow her. I hid all day behind a pushcart until the sun went down.

KENDALL. It's like a dime novel.

SOPER. Almost. I wore a long coat and a vile felt hat purchased from a rag man. I lurked.

KENDALL. Dr Soper!

SOPER. I quite enjoyed it, Kendall. At long last out she came, holding a bowl of what I presumed to be food under a none too pristine cloth. Then she strode off down the street. She spent the evening in a rooming house on Third Avenue with an entirely disreputable looking man in a moleskin cap. Last night I became acquainted with him in a saloon on the corner.

KENDALL. Still in the vile felt hat? You must have made a pair.

SOPER. It was with the greatest difficulty that I avoided becoming pie-eyed as a jackal — Mrs Soper passed a remark, in fact, on my return home, but that is by the by. This man, O'Rorke, told me Mallon came to see him from time to time, spent the night there, brought him food.

KENDALL. Was O'Rorke sick?

SOPER. His health appeared unimpaired. He took me to see his room. Dog bones, broken bottles, banana skins, a rag of sacking at the window — I should not care to see another like it.

KENDALL. Did you glean anything?

SOPER. I did. She will be there tonight. And so shall I, Kendall, so shall I.

A tenement. SOPER tries to speak quietly. He is on the landing. The door opens.

SOPER. Miss Mallon, I have come here to assure you of my good will and to ask you to come with me . . .

MARY. Oh. It's you.

SOPER. Yes, Miss Mallon. To assure you of my good will, and . . .

MARY. I don't know how you sniffed me out and slunk your way up here, but you can bloody well slink down again.

Dear God, every turn I make I wheel around and there you are. Get out to hell.

She slams the door. He knocks, and rattles the handle.

SOPER. May I come in please. Miss Mallon. That child is dying. This is a volcanic time of year . . . we could have a major epidemic on our hands. I don't quite care to shout these things out where we can be heard.

MARY. I don't care who hears. It's nothing to do with me.

SOPER. You have to help us. You HAVE to.(*Silence. He bangs on the door. He shouts.*) See here, I've had a hell of a time finding you and I don't intend to go without saying what I've got to say. You're a threat to society. You constitute a menace to us all. (*He hammers on the door again.*) This is your last chance.

MARY. I'll go to no hospital. I'm well. I'm strong. Strong enough to flatten you, and I'll do it. You're no more to me, doctor whoever you are, than the rats under these floorboards, and I'll flatten you just as surely.

SOPER. If I have to, I'll take you to the hospital by force, so help me, I'll drag you there by the hair —

MARY. Don't you dare touch me, madman. I'm saying nothing. I'm hearing nothing. I'm going nowhere. It's nothing to do with me. I know nothing about typhoid. I've never had it. I've never made anyone else have it. There's no-one in my family had it. There's no more of it where I am than anywhere else, there's fever everywhere, fever, fever, fever, fever.

Echoes of Ring-a-Ring-a-Roses at the beginning of the play swell in and out until the end of the scene.

I don't give a scalding hog's trotter for your stinking hospital

She starts to throw cans, bottles, packing cases down the stairs after the retreating SOPER.

or your stinking Health Department. You're all a lot of black-hearted bloody bastard (*Crash.*) butchering (*Crash.*) murderers. (*Splinter, crash.*) Go boil yourself in rancid scum. (*Crash. Crash. A last shout.*) It's nothing to do with me.

1907 Ambulance (American) bell.

MARY (*over*). In the middle of the night a peacock screamed, my bones caved in. I thought it was a dream. Five men in white coats was round my bed, and none of them O'Rorke. They grabbed me by what they could get, my hair, my thighs, my feet, and hurled me down the stairs and down the stairs while people stared in doorways and flattened themselves like cats against the wall as I crashed by.

Old Knicker Mary chanted by the children.

It was out there in the hot dark street waiting for me as I knew it would, and I knew they'd get me in there and I knew I'd hear the scrape of the bolt, and the bell. Two of them held me down and one sat on my breasts 'till I thought I'd burst with the pressure. I fought them, I gave them a run for their money, it was a wild ride. My heart rattled like the lid on a stockpot — I felt the darkness boil inside me, and I knew it only needed a bit of a stir.

Ring-a-Ring of Roses on distort.

I managed to turn my head and there in the corner with the moonlight full on his face was Michael. He smiled at me, my baby, and oh, it was a grand smile. And then his face, that looked all right, just like his face used to, fell away to nothing.

Sound of an ambulance.

I heard the peacock scream again, they clamped the irons on my wrist; I knew there was no peacock, and no dream, and no Michael, and no hope. So I thrashed and kicked with all my strength, and I bit one of them through to the bone.

A corridor in a hospital. Nurses are wheeling a food trolley and talking softly.

RHODES. Number 42. Hey! Don't go in there. It's the new admission. She's a special. Claws like a hellcat, Bella says. Near bit Lennie's thumb clean off.

ROBINSON. Heavens. We're not supposed to have crazy people here. It's so hot inside these masks — like putting your head inside a basketball.

RHODES. They had to put a jacket on her. Screeching dreadful terrible things, and you know Dr Soper from Epidemiology, well, she spat a big glob right in his face, and he's an important man, Bella was really embarrassed.

ROBINSON. What's she in for if it isn't craziness?

RHODES. Tests. I'll tell you something, though. It's more than just a routine barrier nursing job. It's something wierd. You get to know the feeling.

ROBINSON. I don't like to leave this outside. It'll get cold.

RHODES. With our food, what's the difference. Hash and beans, beans and hash. Rap on the door and leave it.

They wheel on.

ROBINSON. One thing I'd really hate is to have a mad person bite me.

MARY's *room. Willare Parker Hospital.*

SOPER. All right, all right, all right. Let's go through it all again, for the hundredth blistering time. I don't want fine speeches and I don't want lies. You say your immediate family are all deceased?

MARY. Diseased?

SOPER. Deceased. Dead.

MARY. All of them. I was never out of black.

SOPER. Where is your nearest living relative?

MARY. There's none. Some families dwindle.

SOPER. A friend then? Someone that could help?

MARY. None. No time for friends.

SOPER. The truth, Mary. Where were you born?

MARY. In the back room. True.

SOPER. How old are you?

MARY. As old as God. Well, it feels true.

SOPER. In what country were you born?

MARY. I'm an American.

SOPER. You're an immigrant, aren't you?

MARY. I'm a citizen of the United States of America. I'm entitled to rights and freedom.

SOPER. But you are an immigrant?

MARY. So that's it. I might have known. You think all immigrants are trash, don't you. Riffraff. You think we stink — that's why you call me dirty.

SOPER. I think nothing of the kind.

MARY. Stinking transients. We're supposed to pee on the stairs, aren't we, and drink, and kill . . .

SOPER. Mary. For God's sake. I'm simply trying to piece your life together.

MARY. Ah. Doctor. If you could do that.

SOPER. I want you to sit down, Mary, and to listen. Calmly.

MARY. Aren't you afraid, sealed in here with such a dangerous woman.

SOPER. Between us we could get you out of here. But you must co-operate. I want to help you.

MARY. Kidnapped, trussed like a boiling fowl, jailed, spied on, whispers, locks and bolts — that's your help. I'm better without.

SOPER. God give me patience. You are producing typhoid germs every day. They are probably hatching in your gall bladder. The solution is to operate.

MARY. Operate?

SOPER. Get rid of your gall bladder. You have no need of it, any more than you need your appendix or your wisdom teeth. Plenty of people function perfectly normally without it.

MARY. How can you be so cruel? How can you say I'm ill when I'm well, anyone can see I'm well, I'm never sick. Why do you all want to kill me?

SOPER. Woman, I'm offering you good medical care. I'm offering you hope. Will you let them operate?

MARY. No.

SOPER. It may be your only hope of living outside these walls. The Health Department means to keep you here indefinitely. Be clear on that.

MARY. No and no and no. My gall bladder's my own. I haven't that many things, that I can throw them out like old cabbage leaves. And I wasn't put on this earth to provide the Health Department with a bit of sport and pastime. I've a game or two of my own to play. I'll sue the City. I'll get them with habeus corpus. They give me books, you know, that no-one else will read — they bake them . . . what am I doing in a place where they bake books . . . and one of them was a legal book. I know my rights now. Illegal imprisonment. See what the Health Department has to say about that.

In court.

JUDGE. This is an extraordinary case. Dr Soper, would you define for us the term 'carrier'?

SOPER. A person who harbours a virulent pathogenic organism in the body without manifesting any of the usual evidence of infection.

JUDGE. Mary Mallon does not have the disease herself?

SOPER. No, sir. She is immune.

JUDGE. But you maintain she possesses the power of communicating the fever to others?

SOPER. I do.

JUDGE. Extraordinary. Is there a possibility someone may have blundered in diagnosis?

SOPER. I do not blunder, sir. I deal in proven facts. Seven wealthy households, seven outbreaks in seven years, and a single causative factor, Mary Mallon. I cannot comprehend why you will not succumb to the overwhelming force of evidence . . .

JUDGE. Dr Soper, please. New ideas in medicine are always accepted slowly and with extreme caution. It may infuriate us, but it is a blessing to the patient. You look on Miss Mallon, then, as a dangerous woman?

SOPER. Lethal.

Edge out. Fade in.

JUDGE. Miss Mallon, you have been quoted as saying 'they treat me like a leper.'

MARY. Yes. A nurse brings me food three times a day. She leaves it at the door and runs away. They all run from me.

JUDGE. Have you now or have you ever had typhoid fever?

MARY. No. That's what I keep saying. No one listens. Look. I've seen sickness. There's not an illness in the world doesn't show itself. There's such a thing as symptoms, wouldn't you say, sir? Look at me. I'm well. I'm sound all through. I've worked hard all my life, never lain in bed a single day. How can they say I'm sick?

JUDGE. And you deny you have the power of communicating fever?

MARY. Well, of course I do. If I'd killed someone I'd feel guilty, wouldn't I? I don't feel guilty. Let me tell you sir the way I see it, you're a clever educated man, you'll understand at least. The way I see it, there's germs in the air coming at us, blown about all the time from far away places. The wind comes rushing over the side of the earth, up from Australia and China and dirty lands like that, and sweeps the fever all about us in great clouds. So with us breathing in and out, in and out, regular, some of us swallows the germs — that's not to be marvelled at, is it, sir?

Edge out. Edge in.

JUDGE. How long might this tragic state continue?

SOPER. A carrier is not clear until six consecutive negative urine and stool specimens have been taken a week or more apart. Mary Mallon has been in isolation for more than a year. She has continued to excrete the organism, and might do so for the rest of her natural life.

JUDGE. Poor woman. An innocent victim of her body chemistry. Is there nothing to be done for her?

SOPER. The most frequent site of infection is the gall bladder. We could remove it.

JUDGE. A dangerous operation?

SOPER. Not really. Not now.

JUDGE. Then why have you not done so?

SOPER. She will not allow examination, leave alone an operation.

JUDGE. She has refused?

SOPER. Consistently. Rigorously. Inexorably.

Sound of stones breaking glass. Mob shouts. Jeers throughout.
Sound of humming and spoons.

VOICES. Typhoid Mary Typhoid Mary Typhoid Mary Typhoid Mary.

FIRST VOICE. Lock her in the Tombs.

SECOND VOICE. Shut her away in Murderers' Row.

MARY (*shouting*). The Health Department is trying to murder me.

LAWYER. This woman is a victim of circumstance. The outbreaks
   have been without question the result of conditions with which
   she has nothing to do.

VOICES. Typhoid Mary Typhoid Mary Typhoid Mary.

Sound of humming and spoons.

THIRD VOICE. Calamity Cook Kills Wholesale.

FOURTH VOICE. Dear Mary, I have read of your plight and think it a
   sad thing. Would you marry me. I have been ill myself of late, but . . .

FIFTH VOICE. Germ Firm Find Food Fiend In Microbe Probe . . .

MARY. They want to kill me. Slow, by shutting me away, or quick,
   with knives. Either way, I'm done for.

VOICES. Typhoid Mary Typhoid Mary Typhoid Mary.

JUDGE. Silence! While the court deeply sympathises with this
   unfortunate woman Mary Mallon it must protect the community
   against a recurrence of spreading the disease. I suggest she should, in
   her own interest, submit forthwith to examination and to operative
   treatment. Her troubles will not cease until she does. This case has
   gained her notoriety, and this will follow her, and deprive her of a
   means of livelihood, until the doubt about her unique propensity is
   dispelled. I direct the court as follows. Mary Mallon must remain at
   Riverside Hospital, on North Brother Island. Her release is dangerous
   to the health of the community. The court does not care to assume
   the responsibility of releasing her.

MARY's *room. Echoing locks. Bolts.*

MARY (*over*). What kind of a room is this to spend your life in. Twelve
   paces by eight. White walls, white sheets, white faced nurses in white
   masks, all white as a fish's spine. My sepulchre. Through the bars I
   can see mud. Gas tanks. Murky water, dirty sky. At home, the air
   came clean across the sea. They used to say there were more stars in
   the sky than there are ants on earth. See the stars, Mary, how many
   millions, and be conscious of how small and insignificant you are. I
   never liked that. I'm significant to me. Are there more stars in the
   sky than typhoid germs, I wonder? What am I doing here? Is it my
   fault that lives fall about me like boulders? Oh God. Let me out, for
   pity's sake, let me out, damn you all, let me out.

MARY's *room. Several* DOCTORS.

FIRST DOCTOR. Did you have typhoid fever?

SECOND DOCTOR. When did you have it?

THIRD DOCTOR. How many outbreaks have you seen?

FIRST DOCTOR. How many cases?

SECOND DOCTOR. How many victims?

THIRD DOCTOR. Victims. Victims.

FIRST DOCTOR. It's a shrivelling disease.

SECOND DOCTOR. You don't have to die.

THIRD DOCTOR. Do you know what complications may ensue?

Over the following lines MARY's *voice.*

FIRST DOCTOR. Enlarged liver

SECOND DOCTOR. Deep-seated absesses

THIRD DOCTOR. Toxemia

FIRST DOCTOR. Thrombosis

SECOND DOCTOR. Pneumonia

THIRD DOCTOR. Typhoid meningitis

FIRST DOCTOR. Hysteria

MARY. I'm sorry. I'm sorry. I'm sorry for all God's creatures, great
and small. But it's nothing to do with me.

MARY's *room.*

MARY. Libera me domine/de morte aeterna/in die illa tremenda/quando
coeli movendi/sunt et terra/Dum veneris judiquaric/saeculum per
ignam.

MARY *shouting. Banging mug. Repeats dirge.*

Hospital corridor outside the room.

SOPER (*hushed*). How long has this been going on?

RHODES. Been screeching fit to beat the band all night, she's a perfect
hellion.

ROBINSON. She won't be satisfied with anyone but you.

SOPER. I should have been called before.

ROBINSON. I told her right out, didn't I, plain, you've a fine nerve, I
said, didn't I . . .

RHODES. You did. She did.

SOPER. Tie this at the back.

ROBINSON. Expecting a big scientific man like yourself, Dr Soper, to run around. A freezing night like this . . .

SOPER. I feel for her keenly. You understand? Keenly. Lock the door behind me.

He goes in. They bolt the door.

Stop this rumpus. You hear me? Mary. Stop it. STOP IT.

MARY. Oh. It's you. You all look the same, wrapped up like that. Well, now I've a gown of my own.

SOPER. Put that sheet back on the bed where it belongs. Mary. I'm trying hard to hold my temper.

MARY. It's my shroud. My winding sheet.

SOPER. You have seriously disturbed the equilibrium of this hospital.

MARY. Good.

SOPER. Woman, it is five o'clock in the morning. It's cold. Go back to bed, and let me get to mine.

MARY. Don't go. Please. Please. I don't mean to disturb you. I need you for my service. Please.

SOPER. What service?

MARY. For the banishment of lepers. I'm a leper now. I want to do it all properly — I found it in this book — I wear my shroud, and I carry my crucifix, see, I've lit all these candles, and I lie here . . . it's a bit makeshift I know, but allowances will be made . . . and you must read to me what is read to the dead — I'm as good as dead in here so that's simple, but before that . . .

SOPER. Mary, this is impossible.

MARY. You must listen. You MUST. Please. It might work, you see, the service might work in some way, it might please you, or God, or the Health Department or *someone*. You must read the forbidden things. Read them out loud. It's the same calamity for them it is for me, you'll see that. Now. The forbidden things. You forbid me to enter abbey, church, mill, fair or market, or into the company of others, forbid me to go without my shroud, forbid me to wash my hands or any part of me at stream or fountain, or to drink there, forbid me to touch children . . . to touch children . . . or to give them anything, forbid me to drink or eat in company, unless with others like me, and there are no others like me, and if I meet another person who speaks to me, you forbid me to answer unless I place myself against the wind.

Fade.

Hospital corridor.

RHODES. Oh, the heat. My nerves is scorched with heat, comes right up off the sidewalk like a furnace. I'm supposed to go and sit with her apiece. What's she doing?

ROBINSON. Nothing. Brooding, I guess.

RHODES. At least she's not hollerin' fit to be tied.

ROBINSON. Hasn't done that in an age. Just stands at the window all day long. Staring out. Poor thing.

RHODES. Poor thing nothing. I felt sick to my stomach when I was reassigned here. None of us ladies wants to be in there, won't play pinochle, won't play chequers, won't even have a conversation.

ROBINSON. It must be tough. Stuck in there, summer, winter, fall, spring. People staring at her, poking, prying. It's like she was some kind of museum specimen. She keeps her coat on all the time. Says she's waiting for her pardon.

RHODES. She's got a long wait ahead.

An office.

SOPER. God in Heaven, they've let her go. You've let her go.

OFFICIAL. Dr Soper. The committee has given Miss Mallon full instructions on how to carry out a proper hygeine programme.

SOPER. She is poor. She owns nothing. How can you expect people who can barely afford food or the fuel to cook it to boil their water and to wash themselves adequately.

OFFICIAL. She has been most meticulously examined by the committee, I assure you, Dr Soper, and her instructions are exact. She has given the committee an undertaking to forego cooking absolutely.

SOPER. But you cannot properly rely upon her. She'll disappear. Besides, all she knows is food. She has no other skills. You send her out to starve.

OFFICIAL. She has already lost three years. In common humanity surely you would not condemn her to life imprisonment?

SOPER. Yes. It's infernally unfortunate, but yes.

OFFICIAL. Dr Soper, the committee . . .

SOPER. The committee, the committee. The committee is blind. The committee is made up of old men just about spry enough to locate the patient's belly button. They probably vaccinate with a phonograph needle.

OFFICIAL. I see no further point in discussing this.

SOPER. So you're hell-bent on setting her loose.

OFFICIAL. With adequate safeguards, yes.

SOPER. You take full responsibility?

OFFICIAL. Certainly.

SOPER. I wash my hands of it.

OFFICIAL. Very well.

SOPER. Will nothing make you reconsider?

OFFICIAL. Perhaps a public outcry . . .

SOPER. The public. The public's always fast asleep.

OFFICIAL. I'm sorry your opinion of Miss Mallon, and the committee, and the public in general, is so low.

SOPER. Tell the committee, if they saw a mad dog in the street they would shoot it, would they not? Mary Mallon is as dangerous as a mad dog. You will lose her. Sooner or later she will melt into these reeking streets out here. And then. Well. I wash my hands of it.

MARY (over). Look at my hands. Are they any different from yours? Eight fingers, two thumbs. They say I spread disease and death with these hands. It's a startling thing how foolish scientific men can be. I'm not allowed to cook with them, not allowed to hold a dog or a book or a babe. But they're the same as yours, aren't they? This little piggy and all that. They can pray. Here's a church and here's a steeple, open the church, here are all the people. See them all wriggling about, little men and women praying in church, Mary Mother of God, do you not make me like Molly Malone, misbegotten Mary, the moths were right, they knew. Still. No strange marks on the backs of my hands, no devil's kiss, none on the palms. No spreading stains — see. Little crosses — they mean something, I can't remember what. Lines of my heart, my head, my luck, my life, quite long, my life. And here's my destiny. Fate has something up her sleeve for all of us, but she's a very special trick for me. They're letting me out tonight. I'll be free. Standing outside Lacey's with O'Rorke, and the old moon hung in the sky like a banana, strings of windows lit up, steam hissing white from the manhole covers, and all those rich people snapping their way through feasts like barracudas. 'Miss Mallon, do you solemnly undertake to forgo cooking absolutely.' What do they think I'm going to do for God's sake, starve in a land of plenty? I'll change my name, and that'll change my luck. Life would kick you to slats if you let it. But I won't let it.

A New York apartment.

LADY. What time is it, Miss Miller?

MARY. Ten o'clock, madam.

LADY. Oh, my lips are cracked across.

MARY. This camphor menthol will soothe them, madam.

LADY. You're very kind. You must have my tea-set, Miss Miller, the bluebird tea-set. Don't let me sleep — please — you won't, will you? When I sleep I dream. I dream of green arms waving from the water, calling me in. What time it it?

MARY. A minute after ten.

LADY. I'm very cold.

MARY. I'll rub your legs with brandy, like I did with the children.

LADY. I've never paid the milliner for that hat that Otis liked so much. Oh I'm frightened. How are the children?

MARY. Mending, madam. All the beds are in the drawing room, it's like a battlefield.

LADY. I must pay her — debts are so odious. Are the children better . . . what time is it . . . why doesn't the doctor come . . .

MARY. You don't want a doctor, madam, they only harm you, rip you open, bend your bones back.

LADY. Oh, my stomach. Oh, they can't let this happen to me. OTIS! Oh, Otis, I'm so glad you're here, you mustn't let it hurt like that again, not if you love me, dearest. Miss Miller shall have my bluebird tea-set, it's all arranged . . . it's dark. . . What time is it? . . . oh dear, such a pity . . .

OTIS. Oh God, no.

MARY. No, sir, that's sleep. And there's a mercy.

OTIS. I'll watch by her. Sit down. What a night. What a deal of long white nights we've been through, you and I. Battle-scarred warriors, eh? You're worth two of that nurse they sent. Had a fair experience of the fever before, Miss Miller?

MARY. No, sir. Never. Not me, sir.

OTIS. Just know what to do naturally, eh? By osmosis?

MARY. I've not had that either, sir. I swear it. By all the saints.

OTIS. Sit down, Miss Miller, sit down. Rest. Our lives are so giddy I'm going to take advantage of this quiet spell. I know you wish to leave us when our household is restored. Of course, I would have you remain but I respect your wishes. I want you to have this.

MARY. Three hundred dollars, sir. That's half a year's wages —

OTIS. No one cent more than you deserve. After all, Miss Miller, Mary, who can calculate what we truly owe you?

Over train wheels.

CHILDREN. Mary made a seedy cake
Gave us all the belly ache
Fever, fever stay away
Don't come in my bed today.

Mary made a seedy cake
Gave us all the belly ache . . . (*Fade.*)

MARY (*over*). It's a mangy old life. I thought three hundred dollars was a king's ransom, but not with O'Rorke caved in with his chest and me with my hand burnt to hell on an ironing job. Everything going out and nothing coming in. The agencies won't give me nothing. Nothing. I strangle to think of it. Now I stand on street corners like something on the cheap remnants tray — haven't worked in five months. All the way from Dublin across the water to find myself with the same old loafers and loungers slouching and coughing in doorways, slop bowls on carpets of cardboard, pigs' cheeks and bread soup to fill your belly. If you was to give me a nickel for all the lit windows I've passed, framed with brass like a picture, and in them people smiling, chewing, munching, gulping. Food I should have made for them. I should have done it.

Sweet Molly Malone hummed.

FIRST DETECTIVE. We have reason to suspect this woman, Mary Mallon.

SECOND DETECTIVE. Alias Mary Miller.

FIRST DETECTIVE. Alias Mrs Molly O'Rorke.

SECOND DETECTIVE. May be carrying the disease known as typhoid which you may have caught.

FIRST DETECTIVE. Have you been feeling in the last week or two any stomach upsets?

SECOND DETECTIVE. Headaches? Temperature?

FIRST DETECTIVE. Sickness? Diarrhoea?

SECOND DETECTIVE. Let the information go out over the neighbourhood would you?

FIRST MAN. Try the janitor or the watchman. Maybe one of them will come across.

WOMAN. I shared a room with her awhile, 'til my baby got sick and she left. Couldn't stand to see sick people.

SECOND MAN. Far as I can tell she took up with some men; they spent their time running round the city looking for liquor.

THIRD MAN. Try up the street a-whiles.

MARY. (*over, whispered*). Under the bridge. Flat to the wall. Murky here, beneath the brick and steel and girders. Stinks like Patrick Street on a winter Saturday night. Up there the posse that's after me sniff out the city in the moonlight, wheeling and spinning like alley cats biting their own flea ridden tails. Where's my place in the history books? I'm living the life of a yard dog. Year after year of nothing at all. Shall I throw myself in the water and be done with it? No, I bloody shall not.

An office.

SOPER. I make no move unless the request comes from official channels.

KENDALL. There are five letters now, Dr Soper. This one comes as near to bending the committee's corporate knee as I think it ever will.

SOPER. It is a perfectly wonderful exercise in sly humility I will agree. Godammit, Kendall, no. Nearly thirty callousing years I've spent as an epidemic fighter. No. They would not heed me, my experience. It pleased them to think me unethical, inhumane.

KENDALL. I recall you washed your hands of it, sir.

SOPER. I foretold everything. That she would skip. That the world would not be kind to her. That she would violate every pledge she gave the Department.

KENDALL. She must be mad.

SOPER. Certainly she may no longer claim innocence. Five years of travelling about, trailing the fever — look at it all, a Broadway restaurant, a hotel in Southampton, an inn at Huntingdon, a hotel in New Jersey, cheap rooming houses in Maine, Westchester County, Manhatten, all in the wake of "Typhoid Mary".

KENDALL. Do you think you could have found her, sir.

SOPER. I was not asked to find her. I think I could have done so, yes. However as you know my official connection ended when I turned her over to the Department.

KENDALL. They say you are the only man alive capable of coaxing her back.

SOPER. Coax her! As well try to cool quicklime with a glass of water.

KENDALL. So we refuse our help.

SOPER. Well, Kendall. What do you say?

KENDALL. It's a challenge. It's a chase.

SOPER. Hmn.

KENDALL. That's what you used to tell me, sir. You think it hopeless? That you could never find her?

SOPER. Oh, I think I could dig her out. A challenge, eh? It would mean delegating present work, of course. Read me that part about — what is it — 'what we have come to look upon as a major error of judgement on our side', from there, read me that again. I think I might know where to look to find her. O'Rorke. The man in the moleskin cap, if he still lives, might hold a key. You shall go see.

A room in a tenement. A growling dog.

KENDALL. That's one hell of a dog, Mr O'Rorke.

O'RORKE. Yeah.

KENDALL. Does he have a name?

O'RORKE. Yeah. Dawg.

KENDALL. Hallo, Dawg. (*growls.*) Good God. What a creature.

O'RORKE. He's Molly's. He don't like no-one but Molly. She talks to him. Tells him things she don't tell no-one. He's her family. You want some beans? A slug of this?

KENDALL. Thank you, no. Mr O'Rorke, I have tried to explain the urgency — I don't know if you understood . . .

O'RORKE. Don't make no mistake about me, Mr Kendall. I may be on my third bottle of grain alcohol, thanks to your generosity, but I hear real good. Carrying germs, you say. Take her back to hospital, you say. Well. She don't aim to go (*Coughs.*) I'm the one should be in hospital. My chest is all to hell. There ain't a sick bone in her body. Carrying germs, eh?

KENDALL. Yes that's right, sir.

O'RORKE. How come I ain't dead, then? (*Growls.*) And Dawg? What we eat, he eats. How come we ain't stiffs, huh? How much will it cost?

KENDALL. Not a red cent. I swear. Are you expecting Mary, Mrs O'Rorke, soon?

O'RORKE. She'll blow in if she's a mind.

KENDALL. Does she come at a regular time?

O'RORKE. Hell, no. She does what she likes, no questions asked either way. Might not suit the preacher, suits us fine. I'll come home two, three in the morning, there'll be a lump in the middle of the bed. I throw my boot plumb into that lump, it if growls it's Dawg, if it don't move it's Molly — she sleeps like the Rock of Ages. Won't cost, you say?

KENDALL. Nothing. Where will I find her? Please?

O'RORKE. She won't go with you, sure as God made little apples. Then again, maybe she will (*Coughs.*) Maybe she's tired of living this way. I am. Maybe she's sick of running.

Ah, the hell with it. She's at a hospital for women and babies, a lying-in-hospital, about five blocks down . . .

The dog barks throatily.

Sloane Lying In Hospital (1915). Babies grizzling. One screams.

POLICEMEN. That's her. There she is. Mary Mallon.

SOPER. Well, Mary.

MARY. Well?

POLICEMEN. Don't start anything. Take it easy.

SOPER. Here we are then.

MARY. Yes.

SOPER. Will you come with me?

MARY. Oh, yes. I'm too spent to run. I'll come.

VOICES. Typhoid Mary Typhoid Mary Typhoid Mary Typhoid Mary.

VOICES. She shouldn't be in a decent hospital, contaminating people.

VOICES. It's a shame and a scandal the way she carries on, she's off her trolley.

VOICES. Why won't the woman succumb to operation?

VOICES. Not fit for proper folk to mix with. Worse than a street walker.

VOICES. Typhoid Mary. Typhoid Mary Typhoid Mary Typhoid Mary.

MARY (*over*). It's those long lunges of fear coming at me, whispers sizzling like drops of water in a frying pan. I cling with all my faith and with all my bones to food. Food. Where are we in the year? There's ice in the river, the sky's brown as burnt sugar, it must be winter. Apples, chestnuts, filberts, grapes, medlars, oranges, pears, walnuts, almonds, raisins, figs, dates, crystalised preserves. Spare the basting, spoil the meat. The knife should be inserted at figure 1 and after feeling your way between the bones it should be carried slowly in the direction of the line 1 to 2. A thin bladed and very sharp knife is necessary. In drawing be careful not to break the gall bladder . . . the gall bladder . . . as it imparts a very bitter taste. I won't collapse. Oh, the top of my heart's jumping about, all the scum's coming to the surface . . .

Hospital cell.

MARY. Back again. Returning again and again to the scene of your crime.

SOPER. I have no guilt. What's happened to you is what God has done, and there is nothing I can do about it apart from what I have offered already.

MARY. Oh. Fine offers. To split me open. To feed and inject six million typhoid germs into me — hyper immunisation, wasn't that what they called that flash in the pan idea? You're whistling in the dark, I know. I'm not the fool of the world.

SOPER. God decides these things. I can't prevent them.

MARY. A doctor who calls himself a doctor and has no patients.

SOPER. God made me an epidemiologist and you a carrier.

MARY. You're every limb of a dirty dog to say so. He made me a cook. You hear? A cook.

SOPER. Mary. Mary. Try to moderate this need you have for daily commotion. You are a woman. As such you should be compassionate, good-tempered, gentle and quiet.

MARY. Anything I've done, everything I've been, that's nothing to you.

SOPER. I'm sorry. Sorry if I seem harsh. I feel for you keenly.

MARY. But what can you *do* for me?

SOPER. Two things occurred to me — one, you should not have to spend the remainder of your life in this small room; therefore I have arranged for the Health Department to give you a bungalow on North Brother Island, you will move there in three weeks. Two, you should not live alone.

MARY. But I must. They say — you say — as a person I'm out of bounds.

SOPER. I say you shall have a companion. I've put myself in charge. The companion is outside the door, I fancy. I tied him there myself.

He unlocks the door. A growl turns to delighted barks. MARY *flings her arms round Dawg's neck.*

MARY. Oh God, Oh no, oh my beauty, my old beauty . . .

Etc. Ad lib.

MARY (*over*). Dog. A gleam in the dark to me. And the bungalow. A home. Green shingled walls decorated with white trimming round the window, chequerboard window panes. A lawn all round and an elm at the front. A porch. A porch! One large room, a large oak table, an oak and leather davenport, a pressed glass pickle dish, a steel engraving of the Sailor's Return, a rug, a wicker chair, a rocking chair, and daffodils, did he put them I wonder, a bit papery round the edges but still gold at the heart. A bathroom — the water gushes out. A bed with a quilted pane. And in this kitchen, oh I can see it. Tea. A tea of creamed oysters, birds, hot biscuit, two kinds of cake, honey, stewed and canned fruits . . .

Fade.

A laboratory.

During this scene they are both a little abstracted as they study slides under microscopes.

SOPER. When I was a boy I found the microscope held mysteries which fascinated me. Ever since I've been held in thrall to it.

MARY. I read a book on lab work this week. One of the doctors got it for me.

SOPER. Good. Good. You may have the run of my shelves any time you wish. I'll show you later how to keep the records. Now. See if you can focus a slide. Take your time. Mary . . . under these controlled conditions that must be painful to you . . . a thing that would occupy us both . . . I should like to write about this business. We could do something considerable together.

MARY. What will I look for?

SOPER. Rod shaped clusters. Gently. You must get to know it. Unpeel its layers.

MARY. What business, Dr Soper?

SOPER. You. Your life. What happened to you.

MARY. You want my life?

SOPER. Yes. I'd write it out. We'd make a proper thing of it.

MARY. But you've had my life already. Oh. I nearly had a shape there.

SOPER. Once you gaze into its astonishing eye you forget everything, isn't that so? We might make a small sum of it.

MARY. Lucrative lies.

SOPER. Half the royalties to you.

MARY. No.

SOPER. It would be the truth. You should help me get it down. I'm a scientist, not a scribbler.

MARY. No. Is that it?

SOPER. Yes. Typhoid bacillus. That's it.

MARY. But it's beautiful. Like a flower. No. I'll not be flung about on paper.

SOPER. Throw your dollars into the Atlantic once you have them, but have them first.

MARY. I want nothing. I like it here.

SOPER. I thought you'd be happy here. I think you will prove capable. Your hands will be worth two dollars a day to the laboratories — That's equal to the inmate staff.

MARY. My hands? Worth something?

MARY (*over*). As he said that I stood there between the glass walls of phials and flasks and test tubes and something opened in me like the typhoid flower under the microscope. I thought, I've been benighted, I've been frightened to go to bed, frightened to wake, not knowing what I'd wake to. Wondering would they sell me to the bone man for two bits. Knowing I had no value.

And all these scalding fears flew off me, and I looked at my hands, like anybody's hands, like they've always looked, and I was free.

My window has no bars. The days go by. It's Christmas Day today they said but I don't know. You can't stick a sprig of holly on a gas bracket and call it Christmas. I hear the brown river, I see the strip of sky like the old grey road to school heavy over my head. I think of a few of the things I haven't done from nineteen hundred and fifteen to nineteen hundred and thirty eight, swung on a gate, waved a boy off to the wars, kissed a man back from the wars, had a man come inside me, put on walking shoes, danced in gold stockings, rode a bicycle, had a baby, held a baby, bought a thing myself, seen the moon except out of the window or reflected on a doorknob, climbed a hill or a ladder, cut a piece of cake for a friend. But I've been a bit of a marvel. I've a place in the history books. I've had a destiny. That's more than you can say for some. Isn't it? It is. Isn't it?

SOPER. Name: Mary Mallon
Sex: Female
Age: Approximately sixty-five
Diagnosis: Terminal bronchopneumonia of seven days' duration, following chronic nephritis and chronic myocarditis of ten years' standing. The fact that the deceased has been a typhoid carrier for more than thirty years has been contributory.

SINGER (*nasal Irish tenor*).
She died of a fever
And no-one could save her
And that was the end of sweet Molly Malone;
But her ghost wheels her barrow
Through the streets broad and narrow
Crying cockles and mussels
Alive alive oh
Alive alive oh
Alive alive oh
Crying cockles and mussels
Alive alive oh.

I NEVER
KILLED MY GERMAN

by Carey Harrison

For Monsieur Caramello

Carey Harrison was born in 1944, in London, and was educated at the Lycée Français in New York, and later at Harrow School and Cambridge. On leaving university an ABC Television scholarship took him to the Phoenix Theatre, Leicester, where his first play, *Dante Kaputt!* was staged in 1966. Subsequently his plays were seen at the Traverse Theatre, Edinburgh, and the Stables Theatre, Manchester, where he was Resident Writer. From 1973 to 1976 he taught at Essex University; during this time he developed a passion for goats, and an attachment to the more desolate stretches of East Anglia, where a number of his plays are set. His performed work includes nine stage plays, two of which, *Lovers* and *Twenty-Six Efforts at Pornography*, have been published in Methuen's Playscripts series, and some forty television plays and episodes. He is married with three children. *I Never Killed My German* is his first play for radio.

I Never Killed My German was first broadcast on BBC Radio 3 on 9th August 1979. The cast was as follows:

WILLY	Maurice Denham
ALISON	June Barrie
HANNO	Peter Tuddenham
JULIET	Penelope Lee
BISHOP	Stephen Murray
MRS CARR	Daphne Heard
KING TUT	Malcolm Hayes

Director: Shaun MacLoughlin

Silence. A voice echoing.

WILLY. Damn.

HANNO. You all right, mister?

HANNO's *voice is distant. Comes from open air at the mouth of a well. He speaks with a strong Suffolk accent.*

We are near to WILLY, *and begin to hear the ragged breathing of a middle-aged man, climbing slowly down a rope ladder in a deep well, bumping against the brick wall beside him.*

WILLY (*calling, irritable; not loud*). Yes. This bloody torch keeps going out. Better keep going, bottom can't be far now. Dark as night down here.

WILLY's *narration begins. The voice calm, urbane, an educated voice, free of the well's echo, and the irritability.*

WILLY (*narrating to us*). My name is Benefer. Willy Benefer. It's an old name, a familiar name where I come from in the fen country. I don't live there any more. My father was Jimmy Benefer. You'd know the name if you knew anything about silver. Silverware, that is. He was one of the finest silversmiths this country has ever produced. No one remembers him now. We moved down here to Ipswich when I was a boy, to a big house with a field at the back of it, a mile or two outside the town. That's how it was then — the houses have caught up now. I could have sold our field a dozen times since father died. I would, I think, now, if it wasn't for Old Hanno and his goats.

I like to see them out there, in the field. The old creatures. Grubbing around, like me. I could have sold the house and moved to lotos-land. Wherever that is. There's nowhere to go. The world is dying. Why not tell the truth: it's on the wane and so am I. If you could see me, you'd say, there's a cadaverous old face. But I'm not old. I've grown thinner. I live on my own now. Since my daughters pushed off.

The echoes of the well have returned, faintly. Dry, cavernous sounds. No water. WILLY calls up out of the well.

WILLY (*calling*). Hanno? Putting my foot down . . . now . . . can't see a damn thing.

A beat. Sounds.

There . . . it's dry all right, dry as a bone.

He gropes around him.

It's wide too. You can walk. It's like a cavern down here. You can almost walk along. Hanno? Hanno! (*To himself.*) Where've you gone, you silly old bugger?

WILLY's *narration returns without a pause. In the background the sounds of* WILLY *making his way around at the bottom of the well.*

WILLY (*Narrating*). Technically speaking, Hanno is my tenant. Lives in the cottage at the far end of the field. In point of fact he pays no rent. Works in my garden. Or our garden, I should say, because he gets his pocketmoney selling half the crop before I ever see it. Not that I begrudge him any of it.

By no means. Hanno is a genius — nothing less. He'd get strawberries to grow in the middle of the road, if he'd a mind to it. All in all it makes a pretty good arrangement from any point of view. And he likes it here. We make a good team. He prefers to work in silence. So do I. Sometimes I help him with the goats. Then we go back to brew our solitary cuppa in our silent kitchens. Hanno's always been a loner. Though he wouldn't call it that. (*Mimics* HANNO.) I've got my goats, boy . . .

WILLY's *voice breaks in, calling anxiously up the shaft.*

WILLY. Hanno!

HANNO. I'm here.

WILLY. Where've you been?

HANNO. Fetch my torch.

A beat.

WILLY. Ah. Good. (*He pants, calming.*) Well, I mean, *that's* no good. I'm not climbing all the way up for it.

HANNO. I en't comin' down, mister.

WILLY. No no, you stay there and keep an eye on that rope. Don't go away. Just sing out if somebody comes, and try and look as if you're weeding.

Silence.

Hanno? I'm going along the river bed. You stay up top, all right? Can you hear me? I'm just going to do a little ferreting around. Hanno?

Silence. As WILLY *sets off the narration continues.*

WILLY (*Narrating*). He's a good sort, Hanno. But his trick is, he pretends he's deaf. Most people round here think he *is* deaf. So they never bother with him. Five years it took me — he'd been living with me five years before I found out he wasn't deaf at all. Could hear as well as you or I. All that time I was trying to communicate in sign language . . . things like how to train the runner beans . . . madness . . . and cursing him out loud. Till he accepted me, I suppose it was. One day I muttered something about feeling stiff . . . talking to myself by this time, going mad . . . too stiff, can't prune the bloody trees. And he just walked into the orchard and got on with it. And that was that.

A groan below ground as WILLY *bumps his head against the rock. The narration ignores it.*

WILLY (*Narrating*). I say the orchard . . . but I don't want you imagining a great estate — *I* call it the orchard, it's a little knot of trees at the end of the garden. Their branches hang down to the ground around the well, my secret well, the source of all my magic, mine and Hanno's. The source of perfect crops, out of the driest land in England, land so light it drains like sand, which is largely what it is. And as for rainfall, well . . . we've had water rationing here every summer since nineteen forty-seven. Scorched fields. Dying vegetables. Except for Benefer and co. My father sank the well himself, without telling a soul. To make a reputation for green fingers, I imagine, or to cheat the council — round here you're not even supposed to take the water from your own well . . . just a bucket once a day, during the rationing, this is. No more, or you'll lower the water table. So they say. But father studied it, and we're so near the estuary it wouldn't make a bit of difference. All the same, the neighbours would kick up a fuss. So we keep mum. And water by night. And the well never ran dry — it was like a fairy tale. A beautiful deep flawless cylinder of smooth old bricks, like all of my father's work disgustingly neat, the chimney falls it seems forever, down to a subterranean river idling out towards the estuary itself. But at last, in the first week of August, in this summer of the drought, the flow of water faltered, and then trickled, and then stopped. I thought perhaps the pump had failed. Hope against hope. It was worth taking a look — but one of *us* would have to go. I get a bit of back trouble, which ought to rule me out, but Hanno's over seventy, and he doesn't go for heights. He might have decided to go deaf again, if I'd asked *him* to do it . . .

We hear the sound of WILLY's *footsteps stumbling, echoing, along the dry tunnel.*

WILLY (*Narrating*). The strange thing was, I found it the most exhilarating . . . the most overwhelming experience. Once I'd got down there. And the bloody torch went out.

As WILLY's *footsteps come to rest, his voice echoes up, urgent, excited.*

WILLY. Hanno! Hanno!

HANNO (*calm*). Yes, mister.

WILLY. Come on down! It's incredible down here. Come on. The ladder's all right. It'll hold you.

Silence.

WILLY (*calling up*). I've been walking down this tunnel . . . it's as smooth as marble . . . down the river bed . . . there's only puddles, you can walk along it. It's like being underneath the Pole. Extraordinary. I've never come across anything like it.

He pauses, panting.

Hanno?

A beat.

HANNO. I en't comin' down, mister.

Music begins, softly, icy, chaste. And the noise of WILLY *walking slowly, cautiously in the tunnel. Every so often we hear him call, a tuning sound to test the height of the chamber, more and more distantly, moving away from us. His voice remains close, narrating.*

WILLY (*narrating*). It was better, really, to be alone down there, in that awesome silence, in that night so dark the eyes ceased to record the dark and gave off strange lying flashes, like the starfire seen behind closed eyelids, light remembered, brought down from another world. For a time I fought it, calling out to sound my bearings like a bat, by echo. Gradually I let myself be carried, by the darkness and the silence, in a trance, a world all touch.

WILLY's *calls grow fainter still, fade into silence.*

WILLY (*narrating*). Sensing the rock before I felt it. Stopping quite still, in a void, but safe, cradled in space, newborn.

The music has faded as well. HANNO's *voice comes from very far.*

WILLY. Mr Benefer? You all right?

WILLY (*narrating*). Yes, I was all right. Floating. At ease. How desperate my whole life had become, without my knowing it, how stupid. When to stand there, quite still, stock still, with a sense of all the world around as strange and single, comforting and single, was to be soothed . . .

One chill phrase of the music returns.

WILLY (*narrating*). It was only a few days later that I got the card from Juliet. The fatal postcard.

Her voice breaks in, not too close, but intrusively cheerful. Canopy acoustic. Her manner is relaxed, self-mocking.

JULIET. Dear Daddy! Behold, the Bosphorus. Take a good look at the picture. I'm the one in the quilt with a fishbasket on my head . . .

WILLY (*narrating*). She wasn't, of course. But I dare say that was how she looked. Juliet was the younger of my daughters — *is* the younger, I should say. But she'd been the first to leave, to spread her wings, as she thought then. Married at eighteen, to the bearded Rodge. Divorced at thirty, leaving in her wake a husband and a clutch of boys, and taking to the road like some belated school-leaver, greedy for sights. For eighteen months I'd been receiving postcards.

JULIET. The fellow in the headscarf is my bandit lover. Istanbul is Heaven.

WILLY (*narrating*). Scrawled across the postcard with a giant 'H'.

JULIET. Dearest, I've sent you a bishop. I met him on the autobahn — hitching. *I* wasn't, *he* was. Spent three perfect weeks with him. No, not in sin, in Frankfurt. You'll be meeting him. More soon. Strong letter follows. Kisses. Juliet.

WILLY (*narrating*). I hoped it was a joke. It wasn't.

JULIET. Isfahan, twentieth of August. Dearest, bishop on the way. His name is Milkybar, Bishop of Frankfurt. I sold him on East Anglia — he's coming for a holiday. A free Fahrt, as they say in Germany. But don't fret. Yes, I gave him your address. But if he wants a base get him a caravan in Felixstowe. His suggestion, actually. He likes odd people. In fact, he *is* odd people. Speaks English. Mainly the first Act of King Lear, which he recited to me on ze river Rhine: attend ze lordss of France and Burgundy, Gloucester!

WILLY (*narrating*). To calm myself, I went out to my workshop. Began tapping. How could she do this to me? I had my routine, my solitude . . .

Soft, careful noises of the metalwork.

WILLY (*narrating*). My garden. And my growing madness, as it seemed to some. If people called I slipped out. If pursued I could be found among the beehives. That deters them, in the main. I had no time for chit-chat. Besides, I'd taken up my silverwork again, after a long lull. I had a pair of goblets on the way. Difficult work, matching them up. Nostalgic work. Father was in my mind a great deal now. Since my retirement.

The noises cease.

WILLY (*narrating*). I read Juliet's letter again. It prattled on about her Turkish escapades. Perhaps I should have envied them, but in her

flippant shorthand they sounded so manufactured and predictable.
Too gaudy. Too relentlessly unusual, the zanies who peopled her
wanderings, unreal and oddly wearisome, like cheap carnival masks. I
had the strange feeling that she'd never been in Oslo, or in Tunis, or
in Istanbul, but had been hiding out in Cromer, in a boarding house,
inventing everything and getting friends to send the postcards from
their holiday locations. But this one was real. The man was coming.

JULIET. P.S. About the Bishop. His name isn't really Milkybar of
course. It's Melchior. Melchior Geis. Introduce him to Alison. He's
very clean. I love you. 'J'.

WILLY (*narrating*). To Alison. I wasn't quite sure what she meant, at
first. What she was up to. Alison Orde was the one friend I really
cared to see, although she rarely called at my place now the girls had
pushed off. She was very fond of them. She'd been a sort of substitute
mum, for years on end. These days I had to call on *her* to see her, at
her neat little abode. Over the years we met by way of work, at
intervals. Alison ran a little clinic, more or less a cottage hospital,
and I in my capacity as district registrar, and she as matron, midwife,
and the rest, used to incline over the squalling infants, which were
never to be ours. We were chums. We'd both been widowed early,
Alison and I. Alison Orde, née Eastoe.

A beat.

WILLY (*narrating*). Introduce him. Not a bad idea. Pass the wretched
man to her. To Alison.

ALISON. The Bishop of Frankfurt! My dear, what an honour . . . But, I
mean, how will you manage, Willy? Don't they travel with an
entourage? Won't he be bringing acolytes, choirboys with candles, all
that sort of thing?

WILLY. Don't be so silly. He's a very modern bishop. And it's not a
pilgrimage. Here, read the letter.

As WILLY *describes moving out into it, we hear sounds from*
ALISON's *garden, birdsong, a distant jet.* WILLY's *narration in the
foreground.*

WILLY (*to us. Narrating*). I couldn't bear the polite empty face she
set, supposed to please, reading the letter. We could have been
strangers.

Out through French windows I went, onto the crazy paving, to
survey the wilting flowerbeds, littered this summer like forgotten
graves. I had an urge to do something absurd, to practise yoga up
against the trellis-work, my sandals high in the wistaria leaves. She'd
take it in her stride. I'd been behaving strangely for a while, in public
places.

We hear ALISON *start to speak inside the sitting room, then move into the garden.*

ALISON. Melchior . . . what a magnificent name *(Handing* WILLY *the letter.)* There you are. Is that what we call him, do you suppose?

WILLY. Well, I'm not calling him Your Grace, I promise you.

ALISON. Dear Juliet. When *will* she come to earth.

WILLY *(narrating)*. We sat and watched the dog play, on the yellow grass. A dog; a child; it's always a relief.

ALISON. It's far too late to rent a caravan. They've all been booked for months. Besides . . . a caravan? In Felixstowe? He can't be *that* low church.

A soft clink of teacup and saucer.

I suppose he *is* a Protestant?

WILLY. He must have people here, to contact. Various ecclesiastics. Perhaps he'll never come this way.

The sound of pouring tea.

ALISON. He will. If I know Juliet.

WILLY *(narrating)*. She poured the tea, her face intent, a little sharp. Oh, she was perfect; she was funny; she was rude; she was neat; she was pretty.

ALISON. You'll have to get some decent wine in, Willy dear. He's probably a connoisseur, if I know bishops.

WILLY *(pleasantly)*. Rubbish. What I want to know is, how's Hanno going to take it.

ALISON. *Hanno?*

WILLY. You know how he plays up. It's bad enough if someone hails from across the Deben, he thinks they're Asiatics. And never mind just foreigners — this is the enemy. He fought them in two wars. Conspicuously gallant at the Somme, he claims.

ALISON. Bosh. (WILLY *chuckles*.) Bosh as in rubbish, Willy.

WILLY. Not at all. The King waggled his foot in hospital. Hanno's foot, waggled by the King, I mean.

ALISON. Nonsense, you're making all this up.

WILLY. He'll sulk, I tell you.

ALISON. They don't have to meet, for goodness' sake. It's you I'm worried about. With a man of God under your roof. You'll have to mind your p's and q's, you know.

WILLY. And what exactly do you mean by that?

Light laughter from ALISON, *and the background fades, with* WILLY's *narration resuming.*

WILLY (*narrating*). She means my language, and my filthy gumboots, fingernails and hair. My mess. I am in love with Alison.

A beat. The music returns, softly.

WILLY (*narrating*). Last autumn I broke into her house. Nobody knows. I came to say hello, she wasn't there, and I broke in. I climbed the stairs and crept into her bedroom, like a schoolboy. Walked around, addressed the mantlepiece, studied the walls; looked in the mirror; listening. I watched, below, the garden and the trees, releasing stiffened leaves. Nobody came. I left, and as I shut the door I heard the bedroom curtains shuffle in the draught, as though reprieved; standing at ease. Outside it was already dark. The pavements crackled, splintered leaves. I was saluted by drunks. I am afraid of doing something worse. Nine months have passed. I feel it on the way. That night, after we'd taken tea, and argued our my p's and q's, I dreamt a sea monster had beached at Shingle Street, a desolate stretch north of Felixstowe, and I was called to register its death. It was a strange back shiny animal, slick as fresh metal. I couldn't get to sleep again. I was awake at ten to seven when the postman came . . .

The music ends.

BISHOP. Dear Villi! After three weeks, three enchanting weeks with Juliet as our guest, what can I call you but my dear Villi?

WILLY (*narrating*). He came to Harwich, on the ferry. His letter was so . . . friendly, I had no choice but to meet him off the boat. Your most affectionate Melchior Geis, he put, dashing my hopes that he'd sign it 'Frankfurt' with a cross, like the arch-episcopal mark on a letter in the Times. I felt I could have called him Frankfurt. I struggled to pull my thoughts together as I drove to fetch him. After all, it was a straightforward event. A foreign visitor. A friend of Juliet's. Why not? I was filled with the idiotic vision of myself, prostrated, falling to the ground before him, gifted with tongues, and babbling. With the porters staring down at me. But why? I had no record of anxiety in my relations with the Church. A good Anglican upbringing leaves you quite sensibly, benignly sceptical about theology. Alison and I once had a fairly troubled conversation about first and last things, about death, to be exact, in which she was braver than I was, I think, in voicing her fears. And she's skirted the subject ever since. As for me the only moment of spiritual crisis, so to speak, that I could recollect of late, came when I was foolishly trying to move a beehive with about a hundredweight of honey in it, a year ago it would have been, one evening around eight o'clock. My back went, leaving me as helpless as a baby, crawling through the grass to get back to the house and phone Simmons, the

the doctor. Light was getting dim and I was crawling, inch by inch, in the most extraordinary pain, and taking long rests, my face flat on the ground. It wasn't a question of crying out — there was no one to hear me. I just had to get there on my own, back to my empty house, my dirty kitchen, no matter how long it took me. When it was pitch dark, I remember, I'd only got halfway to the backdoor. It was so humiliating, so absurd, out there in the ragged grass like a stricken insect, tired eyes fixed on the distant doorstep, a black shadow in the blackness. Humiliating: yes, not because anyone was watching. But because no one was, not even the grass. So much for a religious education. All the same, I made it to the telephone.

Gulls, distantly at first. Foreign voices, excited, in the background.

WILLY (*narrating*). And now I stood on Parkeston Quay watching while interminable Dutch youths filed onto our concrete, impaled on lurid packs, so many mountaineers. My God — could the Bishop be one of these? Juliet never mentioned his age. Bishops at thirty? Nothing would surprise me. But no, no these were barely seventeen. Prattling away. Bubbling over with excitement. For the first time in ages, I was tempted to a cruise. I saw myself, leering at girls or posing at the rails, ogled by widows. Traipsing round on shore, inspecting other venerable ruins, no, a nightmare, more museums; it was far too late. And the good Bishop stood before me, unmistakeable. A man my age, but a foot taller, gazing pleasantly around him, thin, handsome, with blond hair so pale it was fading elegantly into white. And at his breast a wooden cross inlaid with ivory. A creature so perfectly cast to fit Juliet's preposterous adventures that he rendered all the characters real. Prophets, princes, bishops, bandits. Had she slipped into Wonderland through some mirror of her own?

BISHOP. You are Villi? How nice to meet you! And how nice of you to meet me!

WILLY (*narrating*). We shook hands. I was 'Villi'. I could only think of Willy Brandt with his Bierkeller cheeks; not me at all. Bishop! I said.

BISHOP. Melchior . . .

WILLY (*narrating*). He said.

BISHOP. Melchior. I will not call you 'Registrar'! Your daughter calls me . . . Milkybar!

WILLY. I know. I take absolutely no responsibility for Juliet's manners.

BISHOP. Why not? I love your daughter.

WILLY (*narrating*). The seagulls shrieked at us. The backpacks chattered loudly in Dutch.

BISHOP. This is a very ugly language. In Germany we say that Dutch is not a language, sondern eine Halskrankheit: a disease of the throat!

He laughs pleasantly; he is a very pleasant man. They walk, on concrete. The quayside noises start to fade.

WILLY. The sea looked calm enough. I hope you had a pleasant crossing.

BISHOP. A delightful crossing. I met a young man from Vienna who studied under my cousin.

WILLY. What a coincidence.

BISHOP. I thought so too. Life is full of such accidents.

WILLY (*narrating*). Isn't it, though. When we reached the car I put his bag, a long cylindrical affair, on the back seat. My back gave warning twinges.

BISHOP. Are you all right, Villi?

WILLY. Oh, good heavens yes.

Sound of the car doors shutting: the two men easing into the seats: WILLY *starting the engine.*

BISHOP. I do not know what Juliet has written, Villi. Please do not think I take your time. This afternoon I look for a little hotel. Perhaps a caravan. There are many, your daughter said. I think it will be cheaper.

WILLY. Oh yes. Yes, it would be. But they're mostly booked by now, I fear. We'll fix you up somehow — I've lots of space, at home.

BISHOP. Yes?

WILLY. And I'm glad of the company.

BISHOP. You're very kind. I will look all the same.

WILLY. Even a room is hard to find. The hotels are full of old people. They come to Felixstowe to die. Each summer. If they don't succeed they try again next year.

BISHOP (*amused*). Good for business.

WILLY. Oh, it's a thriving town. Full of fat landladies.

BISHOP. I meant for your business. So many deaths to register.

WILLY *honks the car horn.*

WILLY. There were once. I retired this year.

They go noisily over a level crossing.

WILLY. Do bishops retire? I suppose you don't.

BISHOP (*humorous*). Only to heaven.

WILLY (*narrating*). He seemed a flippant sort of bishop. I dare say it's not uncommon. I found it a bit offensive, all the same.

BISHOP. You live alone, your daughter said.

WILLY. Alone. I have a man, at the bottom of the field. A little cottage there. He's a gardener.

BISHOP (*interested*). A gardener?

The car noises fade.

WILLY (*narrating*). I'd already primed the old boy. Broke it to him . . . slowly . . .

WILLY (*to* HANNO). Hanno . . . I've got someone coming to stay. Just for a day or two. A friend of Juliet's. A churchman. A bishop, in fact.

HANNO (*slow*). Bishop?

WILLY. Yes, a bishop.

WILLY (*narrating*). He looked at me as if I'd just announced the Queen. I — harbouring a bishop?

WILLY (*to* HANNO). A foreigner. A German actually. He's the Bishop of Frankfurt.

WILLY (*narrating*). Silence. He stared at me over the lavender. I feared the worst.

WILLY (*to* HANNO). Now, Hanno, you don't have to see him. It's only for a day or two. I know how you feel about the Germans.

HANNO (*benign*). I killed my German, mister.

WILLY. Quite so.

After a beat.

WILLY (*narrating*). He didn't seem a bit put out. Far from it.

Rising sounds of birdsong in WILLY's *garden, and the approaching car, coming to a halt on gravel. Car doors.* WILLY *and the* BISHOP *getting out.*

WILLY (*narrating*). He was right there by the house when we arrived. Dressed to the nines, and bare-headed. I don't think I'd ever seen the top of Hanno's skull before. Bobbing forwards, sans cap . . .

HANNO. Hanno Tabraham, your Grace.

WILLY (*narrating*). I thought the wretch was going to kneel for absolution.

BISHOP. So pleased to meet you, Mr Tabraham. And what a *magnificent* garden!

WILLY (*narrating*). Hanno glowed.

BISHOP. Such lavender!

He walks towards it, voice growing fainter.

BISHOP. Such roses! Yellow roses. And such Georginen . . . how do you call this —

WILLY (*narrating*). Gushing hypocrisy, I call it, on both sides. You'd have thought it was a memorial to the glorious dead of two wars, not just my back garden: and the Bishop blessing Hanno's penitential labours. Still, they got on. Better that way, I thought, and slipped inside to check the lunch. I hadn't cooked lunch for somebody else for, oh, a year at least. I never cook it for myself. I never cook at all. When I get going in the workshop, say, I hate to stop. And when I do, I'm too hungry to wait for cooking. I just rip things out of packs. You get so lazy on your own. I'm a good cook, too. My girls used to eat and eat. You fall into such awful habits, when you're old and no one's there to see.

BISHOP (*distant*). Villi?

WILLY (*narrating*). Such pleasant habits. Come on, Benefer, pull yourself together. The potatoes are done, and the bish is calling for you in the hall.

BISHOP. Villi?

WILLY (*narrating*). I took him to his room. And showed him round a bit. He was inquisitive, and talked. We lingered in the study.

BISHOP. Forgive me. Your wife?

WILLY. I'm sorry?

Introduce ticking of grandfather clock.

BISHOP. The picture.

WILLY. Ah yes. Yes.

BISHOP. And that is little Juliet; the young girl . . .

WILLY. No. No — little Helen. Juliet was barely two when my wife was killed.

BISHOP. In the war, I understood. She was *killed?*

WILLY. I mean, she wasn't killed . . . by other people. She died. It was an accident. At Arnhem. (*A beat.*) Yes — of all places. So many wives lost husbands at Arnhem. (*He stops, embarrassed.*)

BISHOP (*firm*). Yes. Many.

WILLY. I lost a wife. They sent the nurses in, what they called mopping up. They were parachuted in. They came down in the trees, was how it happened. I was working at the airfield near here. Alfriston. All through the war. On the ground. I never even saw a German, much less fired a shot in anger.

BISHOP. I did not fire either.

WILLY. No.

BISHOP (*after a moment*). Where . . . is the older one now?

WILLY. She's in New Zealand. Married. (*A beat.*) Never writes, the wretch.

BISHOP. But Juliet writes.

WILLY. Yes. (*A beat.*) You've been to England before, Bishop.

BISHOP. Please!

WILLY. Melchior. You must have — your English is excellent.

BISHOP. Thank you, I don't think so. But, yes I have spent summers in England, many summers, before the war. With a family called Wright. In Lewes. You know Lewes — in Sussex.

WILLY. A little.

BISHOP. They are dead now, I understand.

WILLY. You haven't been back since?

BISHOP. Since?

WILLY. Since then.

BISHOP. No.

WILLY. Do you . . . know people here, now? Fellow churchmen?

BISHOP. English churchmen? No.

WILLY. Nobody.

BISHOP. Only you.

WILLY. You must forgive me — it seems strange, for someone of your . . . rank, just to arrive like this. (*A beat.*) Do you travel a great deal, on your own?

BISHOP. In Germany. (*A beat.*) I came because of Juliet.

WILLY. Ah yes. She sang the praises of our native Suffolk.

BISHOP. No. I came because of her. I love her.

WILLY *draws breath to answer perfunctorily: then stops: a beat.*

WILLY (*slowly*). You mean, you love her?

BISHOP. Yes, I mean I love her.

A pause.

WILLY. How extraordinary.

BISHOP. Not so very.

WILLY. Well, no, I suppose not. You love her. I'm sorry, yes. I must be very dense. (*A beat.*) You haven't come to ask me for her hand, have you?

BISHOP (*laughing*). No. No.

WILLY *joins in. A pause.*

WILLY. How extraordinary. And ahh — does she love you?

BISHOP. I don't think so. You know, I don't even know where she is . . .

WILLY. She was in —

BISHOP. Isfahan.

WILLY. That's right.

BISHOP. I had a —

WILLY. Postcard?

BISHOP. Postcard . . . (*Together.*)

They laugh.

WILLY. How extraordinary.

WILLY (*narrating*). *Now* how on earth was I going to get this man out of my house and into rented premises?

BISHOP. I'm sure you find it so.

WILLY. Well, I'm her father. (*They laugh.*) Whatever that means.

WILLY (*narrating*). There we were standing by the door. I could smell the potatoes.

WILLY (*to the* BISHOP). You're her father, too, aren't you — her spiritual father.

BISHOP. Of course. I am not sure if I have made myself clear. I love her. I am in love with her. I have not . . .

WILLY. Slept with her.

BISHOP. Yes, that's correct.

A beat.

WILLY. Yes, that's thoroughly correct. You're not married.

BISHOP. No, no.

WILLY. You've never been?

BISHOP. Married? Never. Never.

WILLY (*tentative*). You are really the Bishop of Frankfurt, aren't you?

BISHOP. I beg your pardon?

WILLY. Forgive me. It's all a bit much on an empty stomach. I missed breakfast this morning. I was . . .

BISHOP. I can show you, look, here, my pass — my passport, I mean.

WILLY. No, no, good heavens, man —

BISHOP. Here, look. I take no offence.

WILLY. No, quite.

WILLY (narrating). He was the Bishop. He took no offence.

WILLY (to the BISHOP). This is all most extraordinary. Why don't — I think — I think we ought to eat. Is that all right with you?

BISHOP. Of course; of course.

WILLY. I'm sorry — we must talk . . .

BISHOP. Oh yes. I hope so.

WILLY (moving away). I've left the wretched potatoes. That's why I'm rushing off. It's this way . . .

His footsteps: and the BISHOP *following.*

WILLY (narrating). We talked about Juliet. Her charm, her vivacity, her bloody awful manners? Her jokey jaunty emancipated-art-school way of speaking? No. Her beauty. We drank to it in elderflower wine. Somewhere halfway through the apple crumble — Juliet's favourite — of course — I'd learnt to cook it with a mother's care — the bell rang. It was Alison . . . the snoop!

WILLY opening the door.

ALISON. Am I intruding?

WILLY. Yes. But it's a pleasure all the same. D'you realise it's almost a year now since the last time you were here?

ALISON. Poppycock. I was here on Tuesday with the cuttings. That's three days.

WILLY. Yes, that's true. On the doorstep — but you didn't come in. And I take it you want to come in today.

ALISON. Is he here? What's he like? Is he sombre and Teutonic?

WILLY. No, he's very nice, speaks perfect English, and can hear every word you say. Now come in and I'll take your coat. God knows how you can wear one on a day like this.

ALISON (warningly). Willy —

WILLY. I'll put it in the study. Out of harm's way. No dirty bee equipment there.

Sound of ALISON's *footsteps, away toward the kitchen.*

WILLY (narrating). I'd mentioned Alison at lunch. And . . . perhaps to keep Melchior company in his dignified anguish, I'd indicated my feelings towards her. Or perhaps I too wanted someone to talk to.

In the distance, voices, ALISON *and the* BISHOP.

WILLY (*narrating*). I'd told him Alison had been a kind of second mother to the girls; especially to Juliet. But once Alison joined us, the good Bishop's face betrayed a mute appeal not to divulge his feelings. Fair enough, I thought. If you're a middle-aged clergyman on a lovelorn quest you don't want everyone to know. And everyone and his cat would have known, if I'd told Alison at that point. Later on, when it occurred to me how differently things could have turned out, had I said 'This is the Bishop, he's besotted with my daughter' ... well, I could have kicked myself; right down the old well. But never mind — the world was heading for a crisis. Clearly, so was I.

The distant chatter fades: replaced by the sound of waves; gulls.

WILLY (*narrating*). That day we couldn't get away from Alison. Melchior talked of searching for small hotels — Alison wouldn't hear of it: we must all go to the sea. And didn't Willy have more than enough room for a visitor? Perhaps she thought he would reform me. I couldn't argue, obviously. So she carted us off to Dunwich. It has always been like this. She wouldn't marry me, she wouldn't sleep with me, and she wouldn't get her hands out of my life. We stood, the three of us, gazing at Dunwich Sands.

ALISON (*windblown*). Down there under the sea, Bishop. The mediaeval port of Dunwich!

BISHOP. Yes?

WILLY (*narrating*). We were up on the cliffs, gazing down at the North Sea and the sand; at a few bathers, beachcombers, at two men with a metal detector.

ALISON. It was a big place; many people; many churches!

BISHOP. Interesting!

ALISON. It all fell into the sea.

BISHOP. How? Fell into the sea?

ALISON. Fell; in the sea. Slowly — many years!

BISHOP. A-ha!

WILLY (*narrating*). Not only did she insist on treating him as if his English were pretty bad — it actually seemed to get worse when he was with her.

ALISON (*still shouting against the wind*). Divers ...

WILLY (*to us*). She was making breast-stroke gestures —

ALISON. Every year; but the water is too fast; too dirty.

BISHOP. Dirty?

ALISON. Full of sand.

WILLY (*narrating*). Next come the skulls . . .

ALISON. Sometimes, they say, the people here, the fishermen — you can hear the church bells under water!

WILLY (*narrating*). No, sorry; the bells.

BISHOP. I do not think so. You think so?

ALISON. When the tide comes in, they say. It often brings up skulls. (*Louder.*) Skulls.

WILLY (*narrating*). Skulls. Catholic skulls, of course, from the great days of Dunwich. Typical of Alison to bring our Protestant bishop to the one scene of Catholic pilgrimage in our area. Oddly appropriate, in fact. And anyway — he was a thoroughly modern and ecumenical fellow. He didn't mind. We gazed along the gorgeous cliffs, to Sizewell power station, that huge up-ended table on the sea; the real source of our strength. These cliffs, these wild roses, were our open-air museum. Above us a painted irrelevant sun. Beside me, Alison, reciting; and the Bishop, greedy for illusion. Their sightseeing revolted me. It was like Juliet's posturing postcards; full of curios. When there was nothing left remarkable beneath the visiting moon. Here was this ridiculous priest, one of Juliet's curios, weeping inwardly for her. And I? No better. I couldn't, wouldn't learn — even from this spectacle. Alison insisted on making us dinner. I got drunk and talked too much.

Sporadic sounds of cutlery on crockery.

WILLY. I want to talk about religion.

ALISON (*dry*). Willy. The Bishop *is* on holiday.

WILLY. On holiday from religion? What an interesting idea.

A pause.

BISHOP. It is not unheard of, I think.

WILLY. No, indeed. Do you still hold a fool feast, there, in Frankfurt?

BISHOP (*amused*). We have many pagan ceremonies.

WILLY. Really. (*A beat.*) What, orgies and things?

BISHOP. In certain quarters, I believe.

WILLY. You don't participate yourself.

BISHOP. Of course not.

ALISON. Don't listen to him, Bishop.

WILLY. Why not? The church is very free these days. I take it you believe in God.

The BISHOP *sips his wine.*

BISHOP. Of course.

WILLY. Of course. What sort of God?

A pause.

BISHOP. I think that, today, more than ever . . . God means different things to people.

WILLY. I'm asking what he means to you.

BISHOP. In three words?

WILLY. No. As many as you like. We've got all evening.

ALISON. No, we haven't. I don't think this is the place to ask the bishop for a free sermon.

WILLY. Free of charge, you mean? (*A beat.*) Forgive me. We've talked and talked this evening — you've talked and talked . . . about the wonderful German economy, the wonderful obedience of German unions, and the unbelievable price of tomatoes. I was beginning to wonder if you saw yourself as some sort of functionary in God's wonder-supermarket. In his wondermarket. Oiling the wheels, you know.

ALISON. Don't be so childish.

WILLY. Childish?

BISHOP. No, no . . . please, we don't argue —

WILLY. Why not? What is God, Bishop? Who is he? I'm an old agnostic. Breathe fire on me.

A pause.

BISHOP. Villi, I am not a prophet. I try to serve people. If I serve them well, I hope that I am serving God.

WILLY. I see. A kind of social worker.

A beat.

ALISON. I should like to change the subject. Tomorrow, bishop, we must show you Ipswich.

WILLY (*promptly*). It's a hell-hole. A ghost town happy in its grave. The only bloody place to be — the only place. Juliet wanted me to move to Wales. And join the herbal idiots.

BISHOP. The . . . who?

WILLY. Herbal idiots. Back to the land.

BISHOP. Ah yes.

A pause.

WILLY. Man on the radio, talking about the land. Last week. About fighting the machine. He didn't seem to think the radio was a machine. (*He chuckles. A beat.*) She wanted me to find a little cottage on the land.

A beat.

ALISON. Why not? You've got far too much room in that house. More than you know what to do with.

WILLY. Burn them all, the cottages. An act of kindness; act of euthanasia. I'm sure Melchior believes in euthanasia.

A beat.

WILLY (*narrating*). It had got out of hand. It was the pylons next.

WILLY (*to the others*). Bring on the pylons. Doesn't anybody understand? Machinery is in the blood. It's in *here. Here!* We wheeled ourselves out of the sea.

A tapping sound.

WILLY (*narrating*). Tapping my brainbox. Them; watching me. They took me home. The Bishop got me into bed. I said to him: I know what you're doing here, Melchior. I know why you've come. To wait for Juliet. (*A beat.*) She's not coming, you know. She's on the run. From all of us.

BISHOP. Sleep, Villi. It has been a hard day, I think. A stranger, a man of nearly sixty years, who knows your daughter, for three weeks. And says he loves her. How can he know this? It is true. I know nothing. I have feelings that are completely new; even with sixty years. It seems to me they are completely new; please understand.

A click.

WILLY (*narrating*). He switched the light out.

BISHOP. Also true that I do not know about God.

Music, the same chaste theme.

WILLY (*narrating*). I slept; a dreamless sleep — or none that I could later call to mind. I would have slept all morning, but for an extraordinary sound that floated through the open window.

BISHOP (*distantly*). Ein-und-vierzig, zwei-und-vierzig, drei-und-vierzig, vier-und-vierzig . . . (*Continuing.*)

WILLY (*narrating*). I peered out. The man was dancing round the orchard in his Bermuda shorts, twirling a skipping rope and counting in that execrable tongue. It was a madhouse. I got up and dressed for my matutinal dip in the estuary. When I came down the Bishop had finished his skipping, and his press-ups, and was chatting up old Hanno about flowers. Hanno had the lovelight in his eyes. Perhaps this really was a form of absolution for his youthful mayhem at the Somme. No, he was grateful for someone who liked his flowers. I didn't; I like vegetables. We argued every year over the herbacous borders that drank so much precious water. The Bishop was bent over them in ecstasy.

BISHOP (*a far off*). Good morning! Where are you going. Villi? Villi! (*Approaching at the trot.*) Good morning, my dear chap! You slept well?

WILLY (*narrating*). The dear chap took him to the estuary.

(*A massive splash.*)

I dipped; he dived. I paddled to the boats; he swam the estuary and back. I'd never seen it done. Golden hair darker in the water, glinting in the sun. For years I'd been trying to get Alison into the water; futile enterprise.

Gentle waves behind. Both men drying themselves vigorously.

BISHOP. Today we find the small hotel.

WILLY. Certainly not. I should take it as an insult to my hospitality.

BISHOP. You will not take it as an insult. I shall not permit it.

WILLY. It is I who shall not permit it, Melchior. You're staying with me. You know I've got the room. And I want you to stay.

BISHOP. I know this. It is I who am insulting. It is nothing that you have done —

WILLY. I've been abominable —

BISHOP. No, Villi. I like my freedom. You know, I like hotels. And I am here to talk to people, and to find my own way. This is what I enjoy. I am not here only for Juliet.

WILLY. Of course not. But you can still do all that. Staying with me.

BISHOP. Yes. But I rather find a small hotel. You will help me?

WILLY. No.

BISHOP. Then I go alone.

WILLY (*narrating*). We went together. Hotels; boarding houses, bed and breakfasts — they were chock-full. The caravans bulged with occupancy. It was hopeless. June was my only chance — June Carr, an old friend. An old bedmate. She owned property in Felixstowe. She always had a room somewhere. We'd slept in most of them; she and I, the widower and the woman of property. I prayed she wouldn't give the Bishop one of those. We traipsed along the crowded sea-front to Carr Towers, as I called it, an unpleasant-looking building with an entire set of whale vertebrae sunk into the brickwork — mocking my patently incompetent spine — relics of an heroic age.

A door opens.

WILLY (*narrating*). Old Mrs Carr opened the door. June's mother.

MRS CARR. Willy! What brings you here?

WILLY (*narrating*). The old crone.

MRS CARR. June's away, you know. She's in Ibiza.

WILLY. Where?

MRS CARR. Ibiza.

WILLY. Where's that?

BISHOP. Yes, I know it. I have been there. Lovely place.

WILLY. Where is it?

BISHOP. In the Mediterranean.

WILLY. Oh my god.

BISHOP. Good morning . . .

MRS CARR. Good morning.

WILLY. This is Mr Geis, a friend from Germany.

MRS CARR. How do you do?

BISHOP. So pleased to meet you.

WILLY (*narrating*). We found 'Mr Geis' a less alarming appellation. This was his usual practice, he said.

MRS CARR (*apologetic*). If it's a room your friend is after, Willy —

WILLY (*quickly*). What about Frederick Street?

WILLY (*narrating*). She gave me a hard look.

MRS CARR (*after a moment*). I'll tell you what. You come inside a moment, and I'll look through the books for you. After you, Mr . . .

BISHOP. Geis. Thank you.

MRS CARR (*to* WILLY *low*). Willy. (*A beat.*) You know quite well Frederick Street's up to its eaves in Orientals . . .

WILLY (*playing innocent*). Really? Dear me. I do hope they're all legal.

WILLY (*narrating*). She fetched the books. A room on Cavendish Street had suddenly become free . . .

Three pairs of footsteps, climbing long flights of stairs.

WILLY (*narrating*). Footsore, we went out again into the remorseless sunshine; making our way past the pier, the model choo-choo train, the funfair with its roller-coaster, past the Charlesworth Hotel, a low white structure with a blue stripe around it, looking like some shell-shot outpost of the Foreign Legion; to the delapidated side of town. We climbed the stairs of number forty-seven.

Sound: the room being unlocked.

MRS CARR. This is the room.

WILLY (*narrating*). We stared at it. Bare, smelly. One old cupboard and an unmade bed. A blood-red counterpane, heavily soiled. June Carr, huge, naked, with her fat breasts, rolled from the sheets.

A sound of sheets.

WILLY (*narrating*). I gasped. There was no-one there; nothing. No June. Only the three of us, staring at an empty room. And children's voices from the street.

Distant voices.

WILLY (*narrating*). I was losing my senses.

MRS CARR. I haven't had a good sweep round yet. As I told you, the previous occupant has only just left.

BISHOP. He left in a hurry, I think. Only half-way through his food.

WILLY (*narrating*). We stared at the tinfoil remnants of a takeaway meal.

MRS CARR. It's the busy season, I'm afraid. I told you, Willy —

BISHOP (*interrupting*). This will do very well for me.

WILLY (*narrating*). I couldn't let him go through with it. The stench, the stains, the broken lino. I dragged the Bishop down the stairs. He didn't protest very convincingly. I was ashamed of myself.

Sound of lapping water: Gentle waves; distant holiday-makers, dogs.

WILLY (*narrating*). We sat on Felixstowe beach, eating ice-creams, in our shorts.

BISHOP. I am not shocked, you know, by this room. I have stayed in such rooms.

WILLY. In Germany?

BISHOP. Yes. In Italy, sometimes.

A pause.

WILLY. You were hitching a lift, Juliet said. When she met you.

BISHOP. Oh yes.

WILLY. You travel around a lot.

BISHOP. Yes. You know . . . quite a bit.

WILLY. And she just . . . picked you up?

BISHOP. No. It was not her car. She was travelling with a fellow from Hamburg.

WILLY. Really. She left him, did she, to go with you?

BISHOP. Yes.

WILLY. Good going.

BISHOP (*amused*). Good going?

WILLY. She found you more interesting.

BISHOP. I think so.

   A beat.

WILLY. You often hitch, do you?

BISHOP. Oh yes. Not so much now, since I was a bishop. It was, that time, because I had given some money to a fellow. I had not enough for the train. It was stupid.

WILLY. You gave him all your money? Who was he?

BISHOP. Someone, I don't know, in the street. At night. (*After a beat, amused.*) I was not generous. I was attacked.

WILLY (*restraining laughter*). You were mugged?

BISHOP (*laughing*). I was stopped. I could not see whether he had a weapon. I rather give him my money. I think I gave too much (*They laugh.*) This was how I went on foot; and because I like it. I met Juliet. So I don't mind.

WILLY. You told her.

BISHOP. Oh yes. We laughed. (*A short pause.*) She is a very happy person, very free.

WILLY. You think she's free?

BISHOP. Well, free, yes, I don't know. She was happy. We went together, on the Rhine. Many places. (*A short pause.*) You can imagine how I miss her. You miss her, too?

WILLY. Yes.

BISHOP. You miss her mother?

WILLY. Yes, I suppose so.

BISHOP. She was similar?

WILLY (*a bit remote*). Oh yes.

BISHOP. You mind if I talk about these things?

WILLY. Not a bit (*A pause.*) Do you love her as . . . a sort of daughter, do you think, or —

BISHOP. No. (*A pause.*) She is a woman. She is thirty-four.

WILLY (*narrating*). We sat for a long time. I felt shaky, after that business in the room on Cavendish Street. I felt as if more things were creeping up on me. As if the pebbles might erupt, to show a head, But whose head? I turned away, to gaze up at the people on the upper beach.

Behind my back, objects came crawling up out of the waves, mechanical objects. I didn't see them, but I knew they were there. My mind was full of things that weren't quite there. Please God. The Bishop was abstracted, elsewhere; on the Rhine. The sun went out, behind a cloud. An apparition in a robe was walking along the beach, towards us. I knew who he was. Please God, I said aloud.

BISHOP. Villi?

WILLY. Don't look. There's someone coming.

BISHOP. Who? This fellow? In a —

WILLY. Robe. Don't look.

BISHOP. You know him?

WILLY. It's King Tut.

BISHOP. King Tut?

TUT (*Distant*). William!

WILLY. He's called King Tut. He's mad; he thinks he's an Egyptian Pharaoh. In fact he's left one of the pyramids to me; in his will. So he says. One of the smaller ones.

BISHOP. One of the pyramids?

WILLY. That's what he says. He's left the sphinx to Mrs Carr. She'll probably go and collect it.

TUT (*nearer*). William . . .

WILLY. Please don't look.

BISHOP. He's dangerous?

WILLY. No, he's harmless enough. He's mad, that's all.

TUT. William.

WILLY (*dully*). Hello.

A beat. The rustle of a robe, the sound of KING TUT sitting on the sand.

WILLY (*narrating*). He sat beside us, sifting pebbles.

BISHOP (*after a pause*). How do you do?

KING TUT *is a man of sixty, with a high pitched voice; genial.*

TUT. Very well. (*A beat; pointedly:*) Thank you.

WILLY. Clear off, will you. I'm talking to a friend.

A silence.

BISHOP. That is a magnificent robe, if I may say so.

TUT. Thank you. It *is* unusual. (*A beat.*) I bought it at a jumble sale. Belonged to an old biddy from Harwich. I think it looks quite Egyptian.

BISHOP. Certainly.

TUT. You think it does?

BISHOP. It looks . . . certainly, Oriental.

TUT. Good. Before I introduce myself I think I ought to ask you whether you believe in reincarnation.

WILLY. This man is the Bishop of Frankfurt. Please don't talk to him about reincarnation.

BISHOP. On the contrary —

WILLY. Or I'll get him to exorcise you.

BISHOP. No, no. I am sincerely interested in such matters.

TUT. Excellent. I'm pleased to meet you, Bishop. My name is Peter Haslam. I'm vulgarly known as King Tut, after my earlier existence as Amenophis the Third. Tutankhamen is of course the only one people have heard of, on these shores.

BISHOP. I too am pleased to meet you. Melchior Geis is my name. I have always been very interested in Egyptology.

TUT. Wonderful. (*To* WILLY.) I didn't know you had ecclesiastical connections, old bird.

BISHOP. Villi is my host, for a few days. I know his daughter.

TUT. Oh?

A beat.

BISHOP. I have not visited this part of England. I came to see it.

TUT. Splendid. And how do you like old Felixstowe? Full of eccentrics, eh? Like Willy here. Old dodderers. You've heard the joke, have you? Harwich for the Continent, Felixstowe for the incontinent. (*He laughs uproariously.*)

BISHOP (*unclear*). Felixstowe for the . . .

TUT. Incontinent. Old people. (*A beat.*) Can't hold their water.

A beat.

WILLY. Have to piss.

BISHOP. Aha, yes.

WILLY (*narrating*). With these words I got up and walked down the beach into the sea. The water was extremely cold.

Sounds from the beach progressively fainter; sound of swimming.

WILLY (*narrating*). I was protected from the first shock by my shorts and shortsleeved shirt. I swam a long way, half a mile perhaps. Looking back at the beach, I could see Willy and the bishop hard in conversation. What did I say? King Tut and the bishop. I could see them, chatting merrily. Why weren't they waving? Why hadn't they alerted the police? The coastguards? Well, perhaps they wouldn't bother. Another old eccentric kills himself off Felixstowe beach. Was I really half a mile out? Was I even in the water? What was going on? I felt dizzy. Fragments of the night before were coming back to me.

I had disgraced myself. In the lobby, at Alison's, supported under one arm by the bishop. I had said 'Alison and I are getting married. Will you do it, Melchior?', Alison had gone white. I said, we're going to live on a pylon, like Simon Stylites. No. What *had* I said? She hadn't phoned today. Perhaps I'd done it now, once and for all. Farewell, my love — perhaps *I* should be waving. No, this was too ridiculous. I wasn't going to drown today. Indeed, far from floating away, I seemed to be floating back. Even the sea wouldn't have me. If you mean to drown, consult the tides. Extremely conscious of my sodden clothes and sandals, I drifted in towards the beach, like my nocturnal sea monster. King Tut had gone. Melchior was gazing at me circumspectly.

BISHOP. What will you do now, Villi?

WILLY. Go home.

WILLY (*narrating*). He didn't seem alarmed by the distance I'd gone; perhaps it wasn't far by his standards. Perhaps it wasn't far at all.

BISHOP. And what about your clothes?

WILLY (*narrating*). The sun had gone. No chance of drying out.

BISHOP. Look — look how wet they are, you silly man.

WILLY. Never mind that. Would you rather I'd gone in naked?

Car sounds, in, slowly.

WILLY (*to us*). Dripping all over the car, I drove him home. In silence.

He eyed me till I could stand it no longer.

WILLY (*to the* BISHOP, *aggressive*). Enjoy your conversation with King Tut?

BISHOP. You think I should have told him to clear off?

A short pause.

WILLY. Don't you believe in anything?

BISHOP. I'm sorry?

WILLY. All this nonsense about reincarnation. You're not a Buddhist. Or do you believe in anything and everything?

BISHOP. I think we have discussed the matter of belief.

WILLY. Have we? (*A beat.*) You said you didn't know about God. Do you know about reincarnation? Or were you just humouring the man?

BISHOP. Perhaps.

WILLY. Perhaps? Were you?

BISHOP. Is that so bad?

WILLY. I wouldn't know. I'm not your conscience. You tell me.

BISHOP. I don't think it's so bad. Even if I do not entirely believe. You think it's bad?

WILLY. Not really; I'm just curious. I want to know what you really do believe. No ifs and buts.

BISHOP. Villi. My friend. You say you are an agnostic. This is what you said. Does it matter so much if I too am a little bit agnostic?

WILLY. For goodness' sake, man, how can you be a little bit agnostic? You can't be a *little bit* agnostic! You're either agnostic or you aren't!

BISHOP. Please, Villi, there's no need to shout . . .

WILLY (*narrating*). We had reached the driveway. I was bellowing. Hanno was watching, open-mouthed, about to drop the heavy shears.

WILLY (*to the* BISHOP). Agnostic *is* a little bit!

BISHOP. Yes, that's correct, a little bit.

WILLY. Well, how agnostic can you *be*, if you're bishop of Frankfurt? I'm agnostic, I'm 'a little bit' agnostic, but they don't pay *you* to be even more agnostic than *I* am!

A pause.

BISHOP. All this because I was pleasant to a man who believes in reincarnation.

WILLY. No! All this because you wear this fancy finery, that great cross on your breast, and you don't even believe in it!

BISHOP I never said this.

WILLY. Yes you did!

BISHOP. No, Villi.

WILLY. Then say it, man. Say it! Do you believe or don't you?

BISHOP. Very well. Yes. I believe in God.

After a pause, the engine judders into silence.

WILLY (*narrating*). I got out of the car, still dripping. Hanno was standing like a statue, gazing at this strange fish, his landlord. Shouting at a bishop.

WILLY (*to* HANNO). Get on with your work. Hanno.

WILLY (*narrating*). He stared at me.

WILLY (*to* HANNO). And leave the lavender alone, won't you? It's good for another week. Don't cut it now. Do something else.

Sound of the shears.

WILLY (*narrating*). He bent and cut the lavender. Don't cut the lavender! Please, Hanno. Hanno? Hanno. Hanno! (*A pause.*) And then of course, I realised. He had gone deaf on me again. At that moment a great drop of rain spat firmly on my forehead. I looked up, and the heavens opened, for the first time in months. It didn't matter. I was wet already.

Music returns softly.

WILLY (*narrating, after a pause*). It blew over, in time; my behaviour, that is — not the weather. I apologised to Melchior, profusely. And to Hanno; perhaps less profusely. Everyone simmered down. But it went on raining. And Hanno continued sullen. And the bishop I hardly saw: he spent more and more time with Alison. Meeting her friends. Dinners; teas; coffee-mornings. Everybody loved him, from the vicar downwards. He was so elegant, so beautiful, and so urbane. I went back to my metalwork; and made a hash of the goblets. A letter came from Juliet; undated; from the Persian Gulf.

JULIET. Surrounded by wealth! And unspeakable sheikdoms. But I need a bath. And money! Should I take a job teaching God's English to the sons of the Sheikh of Qatar? I've had an offer. Well, as you can imagine, I've had several. Will I end up sold in slavery to the harem?

WILLY (*narrating*). Nothing had changed. Nothing would change.

JULIET. Has Milkybar arrived? Isn't he fine?

WILLY (*narrating*). She prattled on about a visit to Mount Athos. How

the monastery air would suit me. But she didn't understand. I wasn't
going anywhere. The trouble was, neither was the bishop. Ein zwei
drei round the garden in the morning, then down to the estuary. I'd
given up accompanying him. Then off on my bicycle and ein zwei
drei he toured the Suffolk churches. When would he go home?
Would he ever go? He would be back for Christmas, he assured us.
Would he leave at all? He talked to me of God; I'd set him off; to
Hanno, of manure. If I was sick of him, I was fed up to the back
teeth with grumpy Hanno. One day I drove up to Bungay and bribed
his daughter-in-law with appalling sums of money, to remove him for
a week. You need a holiday, Hanno! You've never taken one.

HANNO. Can't take my goats, can I, mister.

WILLY (*narrating*). I'll milk your goats, Hanno. And I did. But Melchior
pursued me to the goathouse; while I squirted milk into the pail he
spoke approvingly of natural processes. I could have killed him. It
became, in fact, my chief preoccupation. Traceless poison in the
elderflower wine. Alas, I didn't own a traceless poison, to my
knowledge. I didn't even know a traceless poison. But I could have
stuffed his body gently down the well, which rustled now with
subterranean floods, rushing darkly to and from the estuary. That was
the cunning of my plan; I tested it with a sackful of peastraw — dropped
this floating bundle down the well, and kept a sharp eye on the coast-
line. Several days later I came upon it, sodden, lurking in the reeds
above the ferry. As you might find the body of a too rash bather. I
knew I was insane; the question was, did anybody care: that is — was
anybody watching? Anything? The grass, for instance, or the reeds?
Or God?

The door-bell rings.

WILLY (*narrating*). One night I had a surprise visitor.

The door opening.

WILLY. Alison!

ALISON. Hello, Willy.

WILLY. Hello. (*A beat.*) Come in, come in. We're running a bit late, I'm
afraid . . .

ALISON. You're still at supper? I'll come back.

WILLY. No, no, come in. Zena was giving trouble; we're a bit behind,
that's all. She sat down on me; and then ate my hair. I'm afraid she's
pining for Hanno. Come on in, we've almost finished.

Their footsteps.

WILLY (*narrating*). We went into the kitchen. Melchior excused himself
and slipped out for a constitutional. Did he know about this visit?
Had he, perhaps, set it up?

ALISON. How are you, Willy?

WILLY. Sit down, Alison. Have a glass of this.

ALISON. No thank you.

WILLY. Coffee. Come, a cup of coffee. It's not made of dandelions. Ordinary coffee.

ALISON. Yes, of course. Thank you.

Sounds of WILLY *putting the kettle on.*

ALISON. Are the goats a bit of a struggle?

WILLY. No, no. They're mostly fine. And Hanno's coming back on Sunday.

ALISON. Did you have a quarrel?

WILLY. What, with Hanno? No. He does get on my nerves from time to time. Margaret wanted him for a week, up at Bungay.

ALISON. Really?

A short pause.

ALISON. Willy, I've come to apologise.

WILLY. You? What on earth for?

ALISON. You know perfectly well. I haven't been overly friendly; for a week or two.

WILLY. Well, I haven't apologised myself. For what I said. Whatever that was. I don't think I remember all of it.

ALISON. Oh, it was harmless. I got in a huff. We've known each other thirty years, after all.

WILLY. That's right.

ALISON. Can we be friends again?

WILLY. Good Lord. How could we not be? You know perfectly well I love you.

ALISON. Yes.

WILLY. You do? My goodness me. You've never been prepared to tolerate the word.

ALISON. For heaven's sake, the word! It's not the word . . .

A pause. The kettle shrieks. WILLY *turns it off and pours.*

WILLY. You've been talking to Melchior?

ALISON. Oh yes. A good deal.

WILLY. About love?

ALISON. Oh yes; and about you.

WILLY. I see. I think I see. And about Juliet?

ALISON. Why? Not especially.

WILLY. No?

ALISON. About you and me.

WILLY. Ah. (*A beat.*) To what . . . conclusion?

ALISON. I think I understand you better; or perhaps myself — at any rate. I honestly think I do.

WILLY. Really?

ALISON. I think I've made all sorts of mistakes. Not accepting . . . what you feel.

A beat.

WILLY (*Slowly*). You feel ready to . . . accept what I feel. To accept my love?

ALISON. Ah. I think . . . love . . . is a bit comical. In the end.

WILLY. Comical. Yes, I dare say it is. (*A beat.*) I don't think I quite understand, my dear. We've got to get this straight. If you're not saying you accept my love — what is it you mean to accept? You're not arriving at this rather late stage to say you'll marry me?

ALISON. No. No, I'm not, no. No, I simply feel I should accept the things *you* feel. Not have them bottled up.

WILLY. No. No, indeed.

ALISON. And stay friends, that's the important thing. Without bottling it up.

WILLY. I'm a bit confused, with all this bottling and unbottling, Alison. You sound like my mother with her preserves. We're to stay friends. But I'm to . . . talk about my feelings . . .

ALISON. If you want to.

WILLY. And you'll understand. But not reciprocate. Is that it?

ALISON. That's what *you've* got to accept, Willy. You must accept it. As I do your feelings. With love; with affection.

WILLY. I see, yes. The pill we have here is in fact for me to swallow.

ALISON. No, Willy dear. I've been a cow. That's what I'm saying.

WILLY. Oh, Hardly a cow. A pill, perhaps. Come here and have a cuddle.

WILLY (*narrating*). We cuddled. We'd had this conversation before; it was the pre-cuddle conversation; it was always new to Alison. She was so flushed, and pert and pretty. After she left I was abnormally

depressed. The Bishop was still off somewhere; I went to the shed
and sat with the goats. Did other people in their dotage still say such
clumsy, innocent, evil things to one another? Was it only Alison and
I? How could I know? Who could I ask? The Bishop was my great
white hope — didn't he say the same absurd, apprentice words? *Was*
there a higher language? Or only silence? When I was small, old
people seemed thoroughly silent. Now they were all twittering round
me like starlings. Bishops in love; unbottled registrars; comical
matrons. It was all over. I couldn't go on with it. I was so sorry for
myself I lay down in one of the stalls and promptly went to sleep.
In the early hours of the morning I woke up and made my way out
in the darkness, and across the lawn towards the house. I stood and
looked up; there were no stars. The trees sighed and swayed in the
dark, they too were longing for another life, another go. Perhaps
King Tut was right; we'd get one. But could God be that fair-minded?
An insect squirmed into my sandal; I shook my foot, nearly falling
over, and stamped blindly at it, in the dark. If I'd got it, it lay somewhere there, writhing like I had when my back went, nerve pinched
in the vertebrae, face in the grass. I felt ashamed for stamping at it.
I didn't care much — and perhaps it was only a blade of grass that
had tickled me; I was too bloody tired to care.

BISHOP (*distant*). Ein-und-vierzig, zwei-und-vierzig, drei-und-vierzig,
vier-und-vierzig . . . (*Continuing.*)

WILLY (*narrating*). I hardly got to sleep before the madman woke me
with his skipping round the garden. But when I looked out I realised
he was no longer skipping round the trees, but through them.
Through the orchard. Right over the well; his great muscular bulk
leaping and ducking past the apple boughs. I watched in sleepy
fascination each time he crossed the square of turf that hid the well.
Beneath the turf a concrete lid lay upon a concrete lip; it fitted
closely; and the brick beneath was fragile. If you jumped on it often
or hard enough it might simply give way. Oh yes; most certainly.
How long had Melchior been taking this route with his skipping
rope? How was it he hadn't vanished with a tearing cry, one morning?
Would he vanish any minute? This time around? He came to it. (*A
beat.*) No. He went on over it. Next time? I snapped out of my
trance and pulled myself together.

WILLY (*calling from the window*). Bishop! Not there! No that way —
there's a hidden well! Don't do it there.

The counting continues in the background.

WILLY (*narrating*). He waved and smiled at me, and went on hopping
round and round like a mechanical toy. I couldn't believe it. But he
wouldn't, couldn't hear what I was saying above his relentless
obsessional counting, determined to hold on and reach his century,
his target. I threw myself into my shorts and ran frantically along
the endless corridor and down the stairs; the house seemed to grow

longer as I ran, like something out of 'Alice'. I pounded out, stumbling, onto the lawn . . .

BISHOP. Vier-und-neunzig, funf-und-neunzig, sechs-und-neunzig . . .

WILLY (*narrating*). Stop! I yelled. Stop, Bishop! But he wouldn't; he was sweating, grinning, counting, almost there — coming up once more to the well. Stop!

BISHOP. Acht-und-neunzig, neun-und-neunzig —

WILLY (*narrating*). He was on it, jumping on it —

BISHOP. Hundert!

A beat.

WILLY (*narrating*). Nothing happened. He was just beyond the well now, standing panting, genial.

BISHOP. Good morning! What is it, Villi? What have you done?

WILLY. What have *I* done? In God's name, Melchior, didn't you hear me? I was yelling 'Stop'! At the top of my lungs, man! Are you mad? I said 'Stop!' (*A beat.*) He gazed at me for a moment.

BISHOP (*quietly*). All right, I stop. What is the matter?

WILLY. I'm sorry — you don't understand.

BISHOP. You don't like me to skip? I shouldn't count so loud? I do whatever you say.

WILLY. No, no, no, Bishop — nothing to do with that. I'd better tell you. I should have told you before. There's a well hidden in the orchard. Right in front of you.

BISHOP. A well? Where? I see nothing.

WILLY. You're not supposed to. It's secret.

BISHOP. Secret?

WILLY. I'm not supposed to use it, in the summer. Lowers the water table. But I do; I water when no one's around; and no one knows about the well. My father built it.

BISHOP. And it is dangerous, like this? When I skip.

WILLY. Very, I should say.

BISHOP. Na! I am alive. Tomorrow I skip somewhere else.

WILLY. Yes. Yes please.

WILLY (*narrating*). We stood there, calming, cooling; the Bishop's clothes and cross hung from a branch. He dressed slowly.

BISHOP. May I look?

WILLY. Look?

BISHOP. At the well.

A beat.

WILLY. It's a bit of a slog.

BISHOP. I do it.

WILLY. No, no.

BISHOP. Yes, I can do it . . .

WILLY. I helped him remove the sods; but left the lid to him. He grasped the metal handle in the centre of the concrete disc and lifted it out effortlessly; it could have been plastic. We gazed down.

BISHOP. Beautiful.

WILLY (*narrating*). The water had risen a bit. The drop was still immense; a tiny pool of light, like a hole at the other end of the world, reflected our two silhouetted heads, haloed in blue.

BISHOP. Your father made this?

WILLY. Single-handed. And he kept it hidden all his life. Only I know. And the girls of course. And Hanno. And now you.

BISHOP. Nobody else? Not even Alison?

WILLY. Especially not Alison. Half those people on the far side of the Deben would have their binoculars trained on me night and day. She's the worst gossip I know.

A beat.

WILLY (*narrating*). Hunched over, gazing down, I started to feel sick. I hadn't slept, I hadn't eaten. I straightened up and backed off to keep from toppling in.

BISHOP. You spoke with her last night?

WILLY. Yes. Yes — the reconciliation scene. I take it that was your idea.

BISHOP. No, not my idea. She wanted to come. I am always in favour of reconciliation.

WILLY. Quite.

A beat.

BISHOP. So. You are friends now. Again.

WILLY. Oh yes.

A beat.

BISHOP. She does not love you, Villi. What can one do? I understand very well, I think.

WILLY. That's right. She doesn't love me.

BISHOP. She has said this?

WILLY. It's not the first time, Melchior.

BISHOP. No, no.

A beat.

WILLY. Comical, she said it was.

BISHOP. What was comical?

WILLY. Love.

BISHOP. She said this?

WILLY. Yes.

BISHOP. Last night?

WILLY. Yes.

BISHOP. Ja. Poor woman.

WILLY. Poor Alison?

A short pause.

BISHOP. She has said she is a little bit in love with me.

A beat.

WILLY (*narrating*). My head throbbed. It was full of blood. He hadn't turned to look at me. Still hunched on his heels. He didn't dare.

WILLY. When?

WILLY (*narrating*). I said. Did I say it? When?

BISHOP. Oh . . .

WILLY (*narrating*). When? Idiot; of course; she was besotted with him; ein zwei drei. When, Melchior? Last night, you mean?

BISHOP. Yes. I feel sorry for her, you know.

WILLY. Sorry? You ape!

BISHOP. Villi!

WILLY (*narrating*). Had I said that? My face was burning; it was shining with blood; it made him turn away again. She said it last night? Late? Of course — she'd come to me to clear the way! And he — you — he went round to her — while I lay in the shed and wept. They planned it all.

BISHOP. I think love is . . . a bit . . . comical. In the end.

ALISON (*as the night before*). I think love is . . . a bit . . . comical. In the end.

WILLY (*narrating*). And she was quoting *him!* My head was full of blood. Ein zwei drei. In the end. He had his back to me; ashamed, hunched on his heels.

A thud.

WILLY (*narrating*). I kicked him up the backside; violently. Down he went, a long long way.

A long echoing scream. A splashing thud.

WILLY (*narrating*). Head first. I stood. The birds were very loud. The blood drained slowly from my head. My foot hurt. I felt wonderful. I felt afraid. My brain hadn't returned to life. I peered over the concrete lip into the well. A black shape blotted out the other world; the pool of light that had reflected ours was clotted with a bobbing patch of dark. The water wasn't deep at all. The Bishop had struck bottom. He was face down; he was dead or would be soon. Retired Registrar Accused of Bishop's Murder. Victim Seduced Daughter and Ladyfriend, Jury Told. My brain was back.

No, come, this was no murder case. He slipped. An inquest. Bishop Who Fell Down Well, Coroner Brings in Open Verdict: 'Certain Aggravating Inconsistencies . . .' No, no, I was getting hysterical. What inconsistencies? He came, he saw, he fell head first. The hidden well; that's all. The hidden well . . . the hidden rumours . . . the victim — no — the dead man, seen escorting a certain local widow; she beloved of . . . whom? As was well known. And . . . whose well? Ein zwei drei. But only rumours. But . . . leave it, leave it be, let it drift out underneath the well, a-rustle now with subterranean floods, and when the body turns up in the estuary . . . banged his head, people had seen him dive, reckless. Always went to swim. And disappeared. I could take his clothes and dump them there. No-one seen him. No-one heard us; no-one near enough. As I peered round through the leaves I suddenly saw, to my horror, someone in the drive, in my drive; a figure; Alison. Alison here? At this hour? I stood, frozen, in the thicket, where she couldn't see me. She came round the back, onto the lawn. Peered into the kitchen. She wasn't calling for me? Why? Was she looking for Melchior? She tapped on a window-pane, went in the back door. What to do? Lie low. What if she stayed? I had to face her. With the news? 'Help! Help! He's slipped!' . . . Could I mime grief? Could I? I hated them so much; the Bishop was dead but I only hated him the more for it. I came out calmly, full of cold and hate, and walked slowly to the back door.

(*To her.*) Alison!

(*To us.*) She almost jumped out of her skin. She could have been the guilty one, not I.

ALISON. Willy! Willy. Are you alright? You look awful.

WILLY. Do I? I didn't sleep well.

ALISON. What have you been doing?

WILLY. When — now? A little exercise.

ALISON. A dip?

WILLY. No, no. What are *you* doing?

A beat.

ALISON. Well — I've come for a dip.

WILLY. I don't quite understand. You've come *here* for a dip?

ALISON. Don't be so silly; in the estuary.

WILLY. With me?

ALISON. Yes.

WILLY (*narrating*). The lie was written plain across her face. It was with Melchior. The late Bishop had told her that I didn't go swimming any more; that I was sleeping in; all true.

ALISON. Don't look at me like that. You've been asking me for years to come and share the pleasures of your early morning dip. Here I am and you look quite angry.

WILLY. Do I?

ALISON. Where's Melchior?

WILLY. Down at the estuary. (*To us.*) Oh, it rolled off easy as pie.

ALISON. Is he?

WILLY. I should imagine so. He's not here, anyway. Why don't you go and join him? I'll be down in ten minutes; I need a bite of breakfast first.

ALISON. You look as if you need a good rest. Are you sure you're all right? You're not still upset about last night?

WILLY. Upset? I feel it marked a great step forward.

ALISON. Do you?

WILLY. Very much so.

ALISON. Good. Oh good.

WILLY. Yes. Off you go and I'll join you shortly.

ALISON. Aren't you going to say you're pleased I've come to swim in your extremely dirty estuary?

WILLY. I'm overjoyed; now do clear off. You know I like to eat alone.

WILLY (*narrating*). She bounced off, pleased as punch.

The back door swings back shut.

WILLY. I would certainly join her on the estuary. We would search high and low together. I slipped out across the lawn, cool now, calm; feeling intoxicatingly strong — muscularly, glandularly, physically strong. It takes a kill to find it out: we feast on blood, we humans. I strode unseen, into the orchard. It was safe and close amid the branches. I was safe. At the bottom of the well, the dark hump; and the cross now floating on the surface. He was dead all right. Soon the out-surging tide would sweep out his remains. I picked up the lid to bury them from sight; a searing pain bit like a jungle cat into my back. I fell sideways, still clutching the lid; the lid! The heavy concrete bloody lid. And; yes; my back. My useless, vulnerable and forgotten back. The pain was terrible; I writhed; I flailed my legs like a deer on its side, a great cat's teeth sunk in its spine. I let go of the lid. I tried to move. I was moving. I was pain-free! I was up! It wasn't true . . . I lay there still; the pain was distant — I was paralysed. This had happened for long periods, too — the first time. I had no choice but rest, my mind wheeling like a spun disc on a seafront stick. A stuck insect. We wheeled ourselves out of the sea. A face was looking down at me. Alison's face. Was it real? I hadn't heard anyone coming. How long had I been there? Hours? It was raining.

ALISON. My god, Willy. Oh my god, oh my god.

WILLY. Where was she now? Was anyone there? Had she seen the well? Had she looked down the well? Had she seen everything; the cross; the dark weight in the water? I couldn't see her face. I couldn't move. I didn't hear her go. She must have gone. Or was she watching me? Just sitting watching me; people were watching me. Someone was watching me; some thing. Was I wrong, then? *Was* the grass watching? God, in the grass, watching? But the grass didn't care whether I lived or died; murder or not, the grass didn't care. Yes; now I knew: it didn't care. But it *was* watching. It was watching, parched and dying. Together we shared a last drink from the sky. Madness was in the majority; and God was dying in the grass. Put it in another way; the world was dying; and I was dying with it.

Music

End.

JUST BEFORE MIDNIGHT

HEAVEN SCENT

by Barrie Keeffe

Barrie Keeffe was born in East London in 1945. His plays include *Only A Game* (Shaw Theatre, 1973), *Scribes* (Greenwich Theatre, 1976), *A Mad World, My Masters* (for Joint Stock at the Roundhouse and the Young Vic), *Frozen Assets* (RSC Warehouse, 1978) and *Bastard Angel* (RSC Warehouse, 1980). For The National Youth Theatre of Great Britain he has written *A Sight of Glory* (1975), *Here Comes the Sun* (1976), *Up the Truncheon* (1977): for the Soho Poly Theatre Club, *My Girl* (1976), *Sus* (also Royal Court and Theatre Royal, Stratford, 1979), the *Gimme Shelter* triology *(Gem, Gotcha, Getaway)* which moved to the Royal Court Theatre in 1977 and *Barbarians* (comprising *Killing Time, Abide With Me, In the City*) which was also seen at Greenwich in 1977. For T.V. he has written *Nipper, Hanging Around, Waterloo Sunset* and adaptations of *Gem, Gotcha* and *Abide With Me*. In 1979 Black Lion filmed his screenplay *The Long Good Friday*. Keeffe was Thames T.V. Playwright Award writer-in-residence at the Shaw Theatre in 1977 and the Royal Shakespeare Company's resident writer in 1978. He received the French critics' Prix Révélation in 1979 for *Gotcha*.

Heaven Scent was first broadcast on BBC Radio 4 on 18th February 1979. The cast was as follows:

BOB	Nigel Anthony
HARRY	Harold Kasket
PERCY	John Hollis
PROFESSOR/TONY	Bill Monks
GHANDI	Renu Setna
SHOP ASSISTANT/WOMAN	Eva Stuart

Director: Ronald Mason

The sound of an alarm clock bell.

BOB. One morning I got out of bed and there was this bloody great
juggernaut parked right outside me house. It's only a little side street
and I thought it was right out of order parking this bloody great thing
there and so since it was still a bit dark and being a public spirited
sort of geezer worried about what if it was full of poisonous gasses
and that, I did the decent thing. I got me bag of house-breaking tools
and opened it up. Inside — inside there was about ten grand's worth
of bottles of scent. Way outa my normal run of things. So I did the
natural thing. I 'phoned up the Professor.

The sound of a phone ringing.

Come on, come on — get a move on.

The phone is answered.

WOMAN. Who is it?

BOB. It's Bob. I want to speak to the professor.

WOMAN. He ain't here.

BOB. Where is he?

WOMAN. Honolulu.

BOB. Honolulu — the Professor. He must be doing well.

WOMAN (*heavy sarcasm*). Didn't he do well.

The phone goes dead.

BOB. The Professor being away, that was a real choker. His real name
was Alf King. But he's a mastermind. A real mastermind. Giving
Tony a bell was definitely fourth division, if not Southern League.

The phone rings again.

TONY. Wharrrrrrrrrrr. Who is it?

BOB. It's me. It's Bob.

TONY. Do you know what time it is?

BOB. It's five o'clock.

TONY. Get lost. Will you.

The click of receiver being replaced.

BOB. And I was gonna do him a favour! I took another gander at the juggernaut; its false number plates told me it weren't local. Which suggested it was awaiting collection and if I was gonna collect ten grand I'd better move fast. Pity the professor being away — he'd have had a genius scheme in five minutes. Mind you, Harry was a man who knew where to place. So I gave him a bell.

The phone rings and is answered.

BOB. Hello. Listen Harry son — what would you say if I said eleven grand in exotic French scent?

HARRY. Yes, a little dicky bird told me such a load had been heisted outside Crewe yesterday. But it ain't exotic French perfume — it's fake for Christmas. Genuine foul ponging water with a misspelt exotic French name. Bring it round 'ere right away. How big's the container?

BOB. Get it in your garage easy.

HARRY. I'll give Stanley a bell — tell him to relocate the imitation vintage Bentleys while we unload.

BOB. I'm on me way, Harry.

The sound of a juggernaut engine ticking over.

BOB. Ten minutes later I was on me way so to speak. But being short on diesel, I took a short cut which was a definite mistake.

The sound of hooters and shouts.

I'd forgot the low bridge. (*Shouts.*) Back off — I gotta reverse. Back up — give us a bit of room.

A police siren. Police car stops. Footsteps approaching.

Oh God. The law!

PERCY. Hello, hello — what's going on here?

BOB. Blimey — it's Percy. Hello Percy. Officer.

PERCY. We do seem to have a problem here.

BOB (*to us*). What observation! (*To* PERCY.) Percy, I'm stuck.

PERCY. So I observe — and all this docks traffic building up behind.

BOB. They won't back up and I've got a vital shipment of rare blood I'm trying to deliver to the hospital transfusion centre.

PERCY. I knew they'd spelt the labels wrong, but not that bloody wrong — if you'll forgive my whiplash wit. Okay Bob — we can do business. For a percentage of your takings, I'll give you and the French perfume shipment a police escort. For a grand.

BOB. All right Percy — must be five grand in here . . .

PERCY. All right then everybody! Buck up.

Traffic noises and mix to slowing down juggernaut.

BOB (*to us*). So Percy gave me a police escort to Harry's garage. Harry was a bit upset to see Percy. But Percy was as good as his word and helped us unload after he'd called the nick to say he was pursuing a suspicious juggernaut heading in the opposite direction. Then he drives off to the empty juggernaut with his partner following behind in the Panda. When he'd ditched it in Hackney he reported he'd found it and was commended for his observation and initiative.

Sound of a yard.

HARRY. There you are then Bob — all unloaded.

BOB (*to us*). No transport to move it. The gear stacked up in Harry's garage. I was what you might say Braless in Gaza. (*To* HARRY). That's a bit out of order, Harry.

HARRY. Let's say two grand a week's rent and compensation.

BOB. Compensation?

HARRY. With all this taking up me space I'm out of action til you shift it. Fair's fair. Let's say a grand a week compensation for the vintage Bentley restoration I can't do. Don't look so worried — with Christmas round the corner you'll shift it like no-one's business. (*He coughs repeatedly.*)

BOB. If only the Professor weren't sweating away in Honolulu. He'd have known what to do. In no time. Genius. I now owed Harry three grand. I decided I oughta settle for me losses and try and flog the lot to the professor for four grand. Give his woman a bell, get his address, send him a telegram — in deceptive code — and he'd wire me four grand. In used notes to collect at his bank. The Professor was the answer. Genius — only he could have thought of using a Securicor van to do his bank robberies. Confusion that caused — he was away like a blue arsed fly. And just as I was getting up to get off and phone his old lady — I saw his face! Staring out at me from the local. The Professor had been done. He weren't in Honolulu — he was in pokey. I felt right sick. Turns out he was spotted. He couldn't get hold of a Securicor uniform to use on his jobs — he stood out like a sore thumb in the fireman's uniform.

Sound of a door opening and a shop door bell ringing.

SHOP ASSISTANT. Can I help you?

BOB. Is this where you put adverts in the local paper?

SHOP ASSISTANT. Classified or display?

BOB. I've got something I want to sell.

SHOP ASSISTANT. Shall I fill in the form for you?

BOB. O ta. Twenty thousand bottles of exotic smelling French scent. (*To us.*) So she wrote it all down. These smart arsed dolly bints — their spelling is atrocious. She spelt the scent's name wrong and so it was all legal. Legitimate. She said the advert would definately be in Friday's paper and seven o'clock Friday morning me phone rang.

The brief ring of a phone.

Wharrr . . .?

GHANDI. I'm interested in a cash purchase of the exotic smelling French perfume at a reduced rate.

BOB. I'll have to consult my sales manager. How many bottles are you inquiring after with regards to purchase?

GHANDI. All twenty thousand.

BOB. Bloody hell! Cash you say!

GHANDI. I can have ten thousand pounds in two hours.

Upstairs on a bus.

BOB (*to us*). Outside Harry's place there was a new Jag and a bloke sitting in it with a turban on his head.

GHANDI. Mister?

BOB. Call me Dave, squire.

GHANDI. Good morning Mister Dave Squire. You want to see the money — I'll open the suitcase.

BOB (*to us*). In for a penny in for a pound, (*To* GHANDI.) How long before you move the lot out?

GHANDI. This afternoon —

BOB. Dear dear. In that case I'll have to ask for compensation . . . a whole day without the yard . . . let's say two grand payable to Harry.

A pleasure to do business. I'll leave you to sort out the transportation then. Give us the suitcase.

A pub interior.

BOB. (*to us*). Harry was in the boozer when I got there. He had the five poodles on a lead and he was drinking a Manhattan cocktail.

The sound of one armed bandits.

HARRY. Let me buy you a drink, Bob.

BOB. Ta, if you would — see I don't want to open the suitcase in front of . . . you know.

HARRY. A pint here and another of these. Brochures, Bob — what a lot of holiday brochures.

BOB. I popped in the travel agents on the —

HARRY. A holiday? Greece.

BOB. Kebab land for Christmas. I'll get a temporary passport from the post office this afternoon.

HARRY. Lucky you. Bob I'm feeling very bad, very bad indeed, about . . . I don't know how I can call meself a friend of yours Bob, the way I've treated you.

BOB. A?

HARRY. Letting you shoulder all the worry about shifting the scent. Me not helping at all.

BOB. Don't worry about —

HARRY. I do worry Bob. I can't charge you rent and compensation. That's no way to treat a mate. So I'm going into partnership with you on this deal — equal responsibilities.

BOB. But Harry, it's all —

HARRY. And I'll tell you why Bob. You have problems.

BOB. Have I?

HARRY. You made a tactical blunder. You phoned Tony about it. He wants three grand to keep his mouth shut. But if you're in partnership with me . . . he'll never dare. I've got too much on him. I know all about his saunas.

The sound of one armed bandits.

So what we do is, we open a joint account. Take out what you need for your holiday and then we bung the rest in the bank in a joint business account. You're frowning Bob.

BOB. It's a natural expression when I'm feeling a bit confused.

HARRY. It's as simple as can be. Both of us have to sign a cheque to take anything out. We trust each other. (*Laughs.*) We've got to! What do you say?

BOB (*to us*). There didn't seem much I could say. So we went round to Harry's bank with the suitcase of ten thousand pounds and opened a joint account. The manager was a very nice man. We give a specimen of our signatures each and he gives me a grand in traveller's cheques — for the holiday. It never occured to me to pull out the grand I owed Percy. What with the excitement of the holiday and packing and dreaming about eating a shish kebab and Christmas pudding on the Acropolis and . . . well it came as a right surprise when Percy turned up.

A knock on the door. The door opening.

PERCY. Evening Bob.

BOB. Percy — in plain clothes!

PERCY. I'm not on duty so I'll come in. There's been a complaint.

The door closes.

BOB. You must get a lot in your job.

PERCY. Ever heard of a geezer called Ghandi?

BOB. Bald old bloke in India — I thought he's dead.

PERCY. Not that one, another one. Bloke with a turban who paid you ten grand for the exotic smelling French scent.

BOB. O him. A glass of Retsina?

PERCY. I only drink on duty — listen, I had to rescue this Ghandi bloke down the market. From a riot. People who'd bought the scent going mad when they found it was stagnant water inside the bottles.

BOB. Do for Christmas presents to people they don't like —

PERCY. He was all for pressing charges so I had to threaten him with arresting him for selling stolen property. The skipper — he put me on the case.

BOB. The case?

PERCY. Where the stolen scent come from.

BOB. That's handy, since you're in on the deal. O blimey — I owe you a grand.

PERCY. Two actually. Two, Bob. The skipper knows it's you so he said for a grand for himself he'd book someone else. Tony told the skipper. You shouldn't have phoned Tony that morning — he put two and two together.

BOB. Harry'll skin him —

PERCY. But Harry got wind of it so he's bolted to the Canaries for a while. I'm looking after his poodles.

BOB. That's nice and cosy I must say!

PERCY. So it'll be two grand for me and the skip and the file can be sent back to Crewe.

BOB. I'm off to Athens in the morning — tell you what, I'll write you out a cheque.

PERCY. Make it out to me wife in her maiden name if you will. Only one problem. Harry ain't here to sign it.

BOB. You get him to sign it when he comes back.

PERCY. The skipper's in a bit of a hurry, you know. You know how Harry writes and anyway, seeing the bank manager's a friend he ain't going to worry.

BOB. O, good. Here goes then — different colour biro ink — to look genuinely authentic.

PERCY. Thanks Bob. Bon voyage.

BOB. Plane mate — I ain't going by boat, not now I've got money.

Pause

(*To us.*) As it turned out, I didn't go by plane neither. I didn't go at all. Right embarrassed I was. To get arrested at Heathrow Airport on Christmas Eve. Right choking. Forgery. Cheque book forgery. I got a postcard from Harry this morning. From the Canaries. He says he's very sick about it all. He'll be back in time for me trial, he'll sort it out. I won't be in here for long. If he gets back before the next remand he might bail me out . . . seeing he's me business partner. O, it's cold in here.

The cell door bangs.

PROFESSOR. Talking to yourself again, Bob?

BOB. Any visitors for me, Professor?

PROFESSOR. No. Unfortunately.

BOB. I was hoping Harry might —

PROFESSOR. Sit down Bob. My visitor, she brought me the local paper.

BOB. That bloody paper — it was seeing your photo in there Professor that made me pick it up and give me the idea for the advert and if I hadn't put the advert in the Indian geezer wouldn't have . . . and I wouldn't be in the bloody scrubs again right now.

PROFESSOR. Poor Harry.

BOB. Harry?

PROFESSOR. This picture must have been taken years ago. When he had hair.

BOB. His picture . . . on the front page . . . let me see, let me see.

PROFESSOR. How stupid. Harry going shark fishing at his age, with his ticker!

BOB. Dead, but he can't be dead.

PROFESSOR. Hot sea to drown in, the Canaries. Poor Harry.

BOB. It can't be Harry, it can't be true. He's going to explain — and the money, in the bank, only get it out with both our signatures and . . . IT CAN'T BE HARRY.

PROFESSOR. It's Harry all right. That's Harry. His name under the photo.

BOB. But they've spelt it wrong.

BOB *begins to laugh.* PROFESSOR *laughs.*

THIRTY MINUTE THEATRE
COXCOMB

by John Kirkmorris

John Kirkmorris was born in 1937 in Surrey of Welsh and Cockney
parentage. He was educated at the state's expense in Primary and
Secondary schools.
Since 1970 he has sold over thirty plays to radio, and, to date, has
had two television plays transmitted: *Land of Icecream* and *Printout*,
both produced by Granada. At the time of printing he was working
on a further television script.

Coxcomb was first broadcast on BBC Radio 4 on 27th February 1979.
The cast was as follows:

ELLIS BRANDON	Peter Woodthorpe
FRANK	Harry Towb
BETH	Karen Archer
WALLY	Danny Schiller

Director: Richard Wortley

A theatre dressing-room. The sound of rain, FRANK *polishing a boot, etc. There is a knock on the door and* BETH *enters.* FRANK *hums 'Macushla'.*

BETH. No Ellis, Frank?

FRANK. On his way, Miss.

BETH. There's a couple of script-changes. Would you ask him to look them over?

FRANK. I will that, Miss.

BETH. Bless you. (*Pause.*) Frank, is Ellis on the ball?

FRANK. How's that?

BETH. He's behaving like a sleep-walker — no snap, no sparkle.

FRANK. There's trouble at home.

BETH. Ah.

FRANK. Him and the wife's mother, they're as friendly as two rats sharing a blanket.

BETH. Say no more.

FRANK. Is business good?

BETH. Fair. This rain hasn't helped. We'll run the full six weeks, though.

FRANK. Grand. (*He spits on the boot.*)

The door is opened.

BETH. You won't forget about the script, will you?

FRANK. I'll tellum, Miss.

The door is closed. We follow BETH *into the corridor where*

WALLY *is stacking scenery.*

BETH. Let me by, Wally.

WALLY. Just a minute, darlin'. Man at work.

BETH. That's *Dancing Years* scenery.

WALLY. So they tell me.

BETH. It's supposed to be kept in the flies.

WALLY. Yeah, all except this: six bits of Tyrolean forest. So if you don't mind . . .

BETH. I was only asking.

WALLY. An' I'm only tellin'. Aubrey says 'disperse it' I'm dispersin'.

BETH. Mr Brandon won't like flats in his corridor. I'll speak to Aubrey about it.

WALLY. See if I care.

BETH. Excuse me.

WALLY. Hey, when's you an' me goin' to the pictures?

BETH. Oh, Wally, you are a drip!

WALLY *laughs and makes kissing noises.*

WALLY (*Shouts*). What about it then?

BETH (*off*). Speak to your wife.

WALLY (*shouts*). Nasty! Hold on, I'll come with you.

They leave the corridor. After a pause we hear slow dragging steps in the corridor. The dressing-room door is opened. FRANK stops polishing the boot and rises to help BRANDON.

FRANK. Ah, it's you, Mr Brandon.

ELLIS. 'Evening, Frank.

The door is closed.

FRANK. Take your coat, sir?

ELLIS. In a minute. Were there any calls for me?

FRANK. None I know of, sir.

ELLIS. Oh . . .

FRANK. Give us the hat now. Why don't you put your feet up? Ye've oceans of time.

ELLIS. Yes, I think I'll sit for a while.

FRANK. The water's hot for your toddy. I'll get it for you now and you're not to worry about a single solitary thing.

Pause. FRANK *busies himself making the toddy.*

FRANK. Did ye have a bad day, Mr Brandon?

ELLIS. Dreadful.

FRANK. I'm sorry to hear it. This weather won't help for certain. There's many has a cold at the moment. Maybe ye've taken a little 'flu germ.

ELLIS. Don't try to cheer me up, there's a good chap.

FRANK. Right sir. The young lady left that book for ye.

ELLIS. What?

FRANK. On the dressing-table, sir. You're to change yer lines or somethin'.

ELLIS. Oh . . .

FRANK. Here we are. Mind now — it's hot.

ELLIS. Thank you, Frank.

FRANK. Come, sir, let me have the coat. I can slip it off without you knowin' . . .

ELLIS. I'm completely drained.

FRANK. I can see that, sir.

ELLIS. I don't think I can go on tonight.

FRANK. We'll see how you feel in a while. Now the other arm. There, that's got it! A lovely piece of material. Afghanistan, don't they call it?

ELLIS. Something like that.

FRANK. Drink that now while the steam's on it.

ELLIS drinks gratefully.

FRANK. Enough JJ for you?

ELLIS. Perfect. You're a damn' good sort, Frank.

FRANK. Wheest, it's nothin'.

ELLIS. I mean that. There can't be many like you left.

FRANK. That's truer than you know, sir.

ELLIS. Mm? (*He drinks.*)

FRANK. D'ye mind I told you of my young brother Stevey? Him in the bar-trade?

ELLIS. Oh, yes. What about him?

FRANK. He died, sir — Tuesday mornin'.

ELLIS. No!

FRANK. Thrombosis, sir. Dropped dead in the cellar.

ELLIS. Good God!

FRANK. Like a polled cow, Mr Brandon — five minutes before opening-time. A terrible piece of luck.

ELLIS. And young you say?

FRANK. Fifty-four.

ELLIS. Good Lord.

FRANK. Something wrong?

ELLIS. That's *my* age.

FRANK. Is that right?

ELLIS. Intimations of mortality.

FRANK. Get on wid ye, ye'll live for ever!

ELLIS. I doubt that.

FRANK. The burial's tomorrow.

ELLIS. In Ireland?

FRANK. Not really. Kensal Green.

ELLIS. You'll be going, won't you?

FRANK. I'd like to, right enough.

ELLIS. Of course you must go!

FRANK. They're buryin' um right in the middle of the matinee, sir.

ELLIS. Then I'll borrow Mr Williams' dresser.

FRANK. You won't mind, Mr Brandon?

ELLIS. Not for one performance. Families are important, Frank. Coming and going. Go ahead and make your arrangements.

FRANK. I'm beholden to you, sir. I'll make you sure you don't lose by it.

ELLIS. Fifty-four, eh?

FRANK. Could you drink another toddy?

ELLIS. A half-glass, Frank.

FRANK. I'll have it in a jiff. (*Pause.*) So you've had a hard day of it, sir?

ELLIS. I've been on my feet since seven this morning.

FRANK. Is that so?

ELLIS. Monty phoned me up at half-past six wanting to know if I'd open a supermarket in Kilburn.

FRANK. At that time of day?

ELLIS. No, at eleven.

Sound of toddy being mixed.

ELLIS. They were taping my stuff at the studios at twelve. I told him it was quite out of the question.

FRANK. I should think so, too.

ELLIS. Then he mentioned the fee. It was hefty, I can tell you. I couldn't turn it down. I let him talk me into it. I've been hating myself ever since.

FRANK *tuts sympathetically.*

ELLIS. When I got to this wretched shop the place was heaving with women, thousands of them, blocking the pavements and screaming like the inmates of a lunatic asylum. As I got from the car they rushed forward. The police-lines broke and there was a stampede. 'Ellis, Ellis, Give us a touch' they screamed, and started to paw me. You'd think I'd gone down there to cleanse lepers.

FRANK. Did you stand your ground, sir?

ELLIS. I'm not silly, Frank. I ran into the manager's office and locked myself in until the police brought up reinforcements. Oh, thank you.

FRANK. Slow as you like, sir. If ye don't mind, I'll take your shoes off.

ELLIS. Yes, do. (*Pause.*) The worst of it was I had to disappoint Polly. I was supposed to drive her into Town to her dressmaker. She gave me ice-cold hell, I can tell you, with her witch of a mother chiming in with her three ha'porth of innuendo. Contempt from the contemptible!

FRANK. You get 'em, don't you, Mr Brandon?

ELLIS. How true — in batches of twelve. (*He drinks.*)

FRANK. Can you stand?

ELLIS. Mm?

FRANK. I'll take the trousers, sir.

ELLIS. Yes. (*Pause.*) I haven't told you the half of it, Frank. I put up a black.

FRANK. How was that, sir?

ELLIS. They had cameras at this opening. They showed me with my arms round this fat woman with my fingers clawing at her eyes.

FRANK. Holy God!

ELLIS. I couldn't help it. Those animals knocked me off my feet and I grabbed at the first solid object I could find.

FRANK. That's only natural.

ELLIS. Of course, but the papers didn't see it like that. I made headlines. 'TV star Clouts Housewife in High-street Brawl'. Publicity like that can kill my career.

FRANK. Ach, put it out of your mind. Let's have the jacket sir.

ELLIS. There's many waiting to sink their stilettos into my back.

Crash sounds from the corridor outside. WALLY *has dropped a piece of scenery and hurt his knee. He hops about and howls with pain.*

ELLIS. What the hell is that?

Another crash from the corridor.

ELLIS. Get them to stop it, Frank!

FRANK. Right away, sir.

After a pause the door is opened and FRANK *goes out into the corridor.*

FRANK (*whispers*). What's up, Wally?

WALLY. Banged my bloody knee, didn' I?

FRANK. Can you keep the noise down, Wally. Me guvnor's not feelin' himself.

WALLY. Should hope not at his age.

FRANK. Fair play, Wally.

WALLY. I couldn't help it, could I?

ELLIS *emerges from the dressing-room pushing* FRANK *aside.*

ELLIS. That's not the way. Stand aside. (*Pause.*) You! Shut up!

WALLY. Talking to me, are you?

ELLIS. What do you think you are doing?

WALLY (*mimics* ELLIS' *deliberate speech*). These flats am I moving.

ELLIS. Liar! You were rolling them along the floor. Clear out, do you hear?

WALLY. I don't take orders from flashers.

ELLIS. What?

WALLY. You forgot your trousers, squire.

ELLIS. What's your name?

WALLY. Nicholas Nickleby. What's yours?

ELLIS. Shove off!

WALLY. It suits you.

ELLIS. Impudent scum!

WALLY. Oh, yeah? I'll smack you in the lip, mate!

FRANK. For God's sake, ease off, Wally!

WALLY. Wha' for? He's the one usin' perjoratives — the stupid bleeder!

ELLIS. For the last time: will you go?

WALLY. Yeah, an' I'll take the whole shoot with me — flymen, maintenance, electrics —

ELLIS. Good riddance!

WALLY. — cleaners, stagehands, bar-staff. This won't be the first time you've closed a theatre, Brandon.

ELLIS. Inside, Frank, inside!

The door is slammed. WALLY continues to shout through the door.

WALLY. You want militancy, Brandon? You've got it. My six year-old kid's a better actor than you — you played-out old nance!

ELLIS (*enraged*). Aaaaaaaargh!

FRANK. He can make trouble, sir.

ELLIS. Let him!

FRANK. Shall I have a word with him, sir?

ELLIS. Certainly not. I defy him — and the rest of his unwashed cohort. I've had thirty-five years in the profession from fit-ups to a film contract — I've given everything I've had to it.

FRANK. Sure you have, sir.

ELLIS. And what's my reward? Insolence from flunkeys like that article out there.

FRANK. He had no right to speak to you as he did.

ELLIS. We've entered a new dark age, Frank.

FRANK. True enough.

ELLIS. The peasantry have broken into the chateau and are using it as their lavatory.

FRANK. It's shockin', sir.

ELLIS. I won't be able to perform tonight — look at my hands.

FRANK. Your poor nerves are jumpin'. A wee whiskey could settle them. Sit ye down while I fetch it.

ELLIS. Did you hear what that lout called me, Frank? A 'nance'.

FRANK. Take no notice, sir.

ELLIS. I may not be the greatest lover of all time but three wives ought to count for something.

The sound of whiskey being poured.

FRANK. Must do.

ELLIS. Mind you, I've nothing in principle against fairies. Some of my oldest and closest friends . . . (*He coughs realising what he is about to say.*) That was damned wounding.

FRANK. See that away, sir.

ELLIS. I'm an artist. I need repose, I have to nourish my craft. Without relaxation, I'm lost.

FRANK. Cheers, Mr Brandon.

ELLIS. This schedule's killing me: studios in the morning; eight performances a week here, the guest-appearances —

FRANK. Take your drink, sir.

ELLIS. I haven't slept properly in months.

FRANK. That's a terrible thing.

ELLIS. And when I do manage to drop off it's only to dream of my dead. (*Pause.*) Good health. (*Drinks.*)

Long pause.

FRANK. Is that better?

ELLIS. Lots, thank you, Frank.

FRANK. Shall we start on your make-up?

ELLIS. I'm not going on.

FRANK. So you said, sir. But you always feel better with yer warpaint on, don't you? Come, I'll take your shirt . . .

ELLIS. All right, all right. Take the booze then —

Long pause.

ELLIS. Talking of the dead, I saw Hal Ramsay yesterday.

FRANK. The fillum-star?

ELLIS. It's been a long time since he was that. I went out to buy a paper in the morning and I was a walking back through the park. I saw this dessicated old man running round the paths in a moth-eaten leotard. I thought I recognised him. It was Hal all right — no hair, brown as a wardrobe. He didn't recognise me.

FRANK. I dressed for um once. A very nice man.

ELLIS. Yes, and a first-rate actor. I ought to have stopped him and shaken his hand. Why didn't I, Frank? (*Pause.*) I don't believe I'm a very pleasant fellow.

FRANK. Let me tuck the towel in.

ELLIS. Hal shared digs with me in Sunderland once. We've often dismembered one fish-supper between us and fought over the crispy bits. (*Laughs.*)

FRANK. Happy days, sir!

ELLIS. Happy? They were horrible Frank. God, how I hated being poor!

There is a knock on the door and it opens.

BETH. May I come in, Ellis?

ELLIS. No. Frank, another towel. This one has lumps in it.

BETH. I'd rather like to talk, Ellis.

ELLIS. No point. I know in advance what you'll say. It's about that *canaille* and their filthy scenery.

BETH (*whispers*). They'll hear you!

ELLIS. Then close the door. Doors impede hearing, you know . . .

She closes the door.

Very well, what do you have to say?

BETH. The stagehands are close to mutiny, Ellis.

ELLIS. Shoot them down then.

BETH. The chap you had the argument with is closing the theatre.

ELLIS. Crude bluff, dearie.

BETH. It's not — he's the convenor.

ELLIS. My dear child, I don't care if he's the High Priest of Egypt.

BETH. He means it, Ellis.

ELLIS. Those understrappers are wagging the wrong end of the dog. I think I can claim it's my presence which is filling those benches in the auditorium.

BETH. Nobody doubts that, Ellis.

ELLIS. Then why may I not have a proper atmosphere in which to do my work?

BETH. It's very vexing, I know.

ELLIS. You have a notable gift for understatement.

BETH. Couldn't you persuade them to stay?

ELLIS. What? Wheedle, crawl? What of my self-respect — my dignity? What are you smirking at? (*Pause.*) Oh. Frank, my robe.

BETH *supresses a giggle.*

You've seen a mummer in his pelt before, haven't you? It's a poor comment on the times when the victim has to apologise for the way he's been treated.

BETH. That's it exactly: *we* know you're in the right — *they* don't. By apologising you put one over on them.

ELLIS. Spoken like a Jesuit! All right, I'll do it.

BETH. Thanks, Ellis, you're a pet.

ELLIS. I know.

FRANK. Your robe, Mr Brandon.

BETH *opens the door.*

BETH (*softly, off*). Wally, will you come in?

Long pause.

ELLIS. Don't be bashful — all the way in.

Pause. The door is closed.

BETH. Ellis, this is Wally Tyler.

ELLIS (*drily*). Mr Tyler and I have already introduced ourselves.

WALLY. No persiflage if you don't mind, Brandon. A few minutes ago you villified me in public. Paddy here is my independant witness. Unless an apology in the due form is forthcoming I'm going to put the blocks on tonight's performance. What's your response to that?

ELLIS. Puzzlement. Dismay . . . Shock. I'm surprised a small remonstration on my part should provoke such a weight of flak. I have had an exhausting day — no excuse for churlish conduct, I grant you. I regret our contretemps and hope you will withdraw your sanctions.

WALLY. Pardon?

ELLIS. I'm sorry, Mr Tyler, deeply, humbly sorry.

WALLY. That's all right then. I accept the apology, conditional on your future behaviour.

ELLIS (*grits teeth*). I shall try, Mr Tyler. And in the same spirit I hope you will as the French have it, *baisez mon cou.*

WALLY. That's okay.

ELLIS. And as often as you have a mind to. Now may I offer you some refreshment?

WALLY. I decline. The labouring classes aren't to be bought off with the opiates of the upper middles.

ELLIS. Excuse my presumption.

WALLY. Yeah. You watch it, Brandon, we haven't finished with each other. Okay, darlin', the show — for what it's worth — goes on.

The door opens and after a pause, is closed.

ELLIS (*venting rage*). Aaaaaargh!

BETH. It was galling but you were magnificent, Ellis.

ELLIS. Tell me, is this a theatre or the battleship Potemkin?

BETH. I must go. Thanks a heap for the co-operation.

She opens the door.

Did you . . .?

ELLIS. What?

BETH. It's not important. 'Bye!

She closes the door.

ELLIS. What a modest jolly little thing she is. What a crook!

FRANK. She's right, sir. You handled yourself like a statesman. We ought to be starting on our face, sir. Come and sit ye down.

Long pause.

ELLIS. Why doesn't my wife call?

FRANK. Early days, sir.

ELLIS. I hate to leave her in a huff. Is this all the base I've left?

FRANK. There's more in the drawer, sir. I'll —

ELLIS. No, I'll get it.

He opens the drawer.

You're not married, are you, Frank?

FRANK. I never had the pleasure, no.

ELLIS. Take a tip from an old hand — don't. And if you find you can't help yourself never marry a woman whose mother was in variety.

FRANK. I'll remember, sir.

ELLIS. My very own crone-in-residence refers to herself as an artiste, appropriate for a magician's assistant. Lebeau and Belle, Illusionists Supreme. Spent her career jumping out of boxes with a smirk on her face and a powder puff pinned to her backside. Now you see her, now you don't. I wish to God I never had.

FRANK. (*laughs*). Is it the silk or the cloth tonight?

ELLIS. Silk, please. When Poll asked me if we could put up Mumsy for a few days I walked right into it. A few days! We're into the eleventh soul-searing month.

FRANK. Well I never!

ELLIS. Every minute weighs like a boulder on my heart. And when I suggested to Polly — in the most delicate way imaginable — that Mumsy slung her hook, she curtailed my privileges for a fortnight.

FRANK *tuts sympathetically.*

I hope I'm not a mean sort, Frank —

FRANK. That you're not.

ELLIS. But between them they're breaking me. Charge accounts, dress bills, little jaunts to Paris. And the drink! Vera guzzles gin as it if were milk — I've seen her put away a bottle in an hour and a quarter and all it did was raise sweat on her upper lip.

FRANK. Your shirt, sir. Ruffles or plain?

ELLIS (*ponders*). Plain first, ruffles for the last act. (*Pause.*) Polly's a dear girl and I adore her, but she's obsessed with her looks.

FRANK. Mrs B's a fine handsome young woman, right enough.

ELLIS. Which I'm never tired of telling her. But she spends three days a week having herself titivated by this hair-cutter in Knightsbridge. Calls himself Gino. He's no Gino; he a Glaswegian called M'Gurk, I checked. Don't be misled by propaganda, Frank, the ladies' barbers aren't all limp wristed. She said the most extraordinary thing to me about this man this morning: he'd advised her to have her bosoms lifted.

FRANK. Isn't that painful, sir?

ELLIS. She meant surgically. Of course, a tiny question insinuated itself into my mind: what business has this Caledonian-Gino evaluating my wife's chest?

FRANK. It makes you think, sir.

ELLIS. Right!

FRANK. Shall I start dressing you, sir?

ELLIS. Why not? I do believe I'm perking up a little.

FRANK. Wasn't I saying so only a quarter of an hour ago?

ELLIS. Bring that script with you, will you? (*Pause.*) I know where she is at this minute. She's at home sitting by the telephone table while her mother pours poison into her ear and alcohol down her own wide gullet. Polly knows I worry. It's a game. If I call it means I don't trust her, but if I don't, I don't care which is equally untrue but can't be proved. Don't marry, Frank.

FRANK. Your script. And your shirt.

The script rustles.

ELLIS. Have you seen the play, Frank?

FRANK. Not all the way through, sir.

ELLIS. It's filthy.

FRANK. Isn't it a classic?

ELLIS. A bawdy classic, Frank. But it's good honest filth, not like this tacky modern stuff. It has style and wit. Of course you can't understand everything that's said, otherwise it wouldn't be a classic.

The sound of the script's pages being turned.

FRANK. There. We're ready for the breeches.

ELLIS. What's this? What? I'll be shot first!

FRANK. What is it, sir?

ELLIS. They've cut my part! Look — blue pencil. Only my best lines, too. And a note from Mr Aubrey Schwarz. 'In the interests of the team would I consent . . .' There's my answer.

The sound of paper tearing.

ELLIS. Aubrey Schwarz may be the greatest *metteur-en-scene* since Rheinhardt — which he isn't — but he knows sweet damn-all about literature!

FRANK. Yer breeches, Mr Brandon.

ELLIS. No wonder the nation's in its present plight. We've lost our intestinal fortitude. What can you expect from a people that stuffs itself with sliced white bread?

FRANK. What indeed?

ELLIS. No heart, no bowels, no breeding!

FRANK. It's a great shame. Can you button up, sir?

ELLIS. I'll leave the top one undone. Have to cut down on the spuds for a few weeks.

FRANK. If yer ready, we'll get in to the boots.

ELLIS. How are we for time?

FRANK. Running nicely up to the starting-gate. Right, sir, grab my shoulder.

ELLIS. Be gentle with me, Frank.

FRANK. You can do it, sir.

ELLIS. Eight times a week! I'd rather have a tooth pulled.

FRANK. Push!

ELLIS screams and groans.

FRANK. Luveley. Now the other.

ELLIS. Wait, wait! I'm out of breath. (*Pause.*) Now!

ELLIS groans again.

FRANK. Stamp your feet, sir.

ELLIS, *groaning, obeys him.*

There, a beautiful fit.

ELLIS. I can't feel my toes.

FRANK. Walk around a bit, sir. The blood'll come back.

ELLIS clumps around the dressing-room.

No doubt about it, Mr Brandon, you were born to sit a horse.

ELLIS. I loathe horses.

FRANK. Shall I coat and wig ye?

ELLIS. All right.

The telephone rings.

FRANK. Shall I . . .?

ELLIS. Would you?

Pause. The receiver is lifted, FRANK *speaks in a low voice into the telephone.*

FRANK (*into the phone*). Mr Brandon's dressing-room. Who? Would you hold the line, please. (*Whispers.*) The wife's mother, sir! Will you speak to her?

ELLIS. Tell her I'm in the lavatory.

FRANK (*into the phone*). I'm sorry, he's unavailable at the moment. You'll wait? He's liable to be a long time . . .

ELLIS. Give it here, Frank. (*Pause. He speaks into the phone.*) Vera, my love! I was detained upstairs. What? But what do you expect me to do? Call the engineers, dear. Their number's in the book. The little black book by your elbow. Is — is — um — Polly there? Where? No, it's not important. I have to go, Vera. No, I can't chat. The black book — under T for Television. T, dear — as in tight. Yes, Vera, goodbye.

The telephone is replaced.

There's smoke pouring from the television-set. I'm not surprised. She never gives it time to cool down. Weskit and wig, Frank.

FRANK. Right, sir.

ELLIS. My wife is dining with friends.

FRANK. Then that's all right, isn't it?

ELLIS. Not altogether. Those particular friends happen to be in South America. But, not to worry. In Vera's condition all names sound alike. No, I'll button it. My tool, Frank.

FRANK. Sir?

ELLIS. My blade, Frank, my rapier.

FRANK. Ready and waitin'.

ELLIS. Did you let out the strap?

FRANK. One hole, that should do it.

ELLIS. Come on, come on — I'm not dressed without my weaponry.

FRANK. It could do with a bit polishin'.

ELLIS. Later, Frank. I think I'll limber up with a few passes.

The sword rings as it's withdrawn from its scabbard.

FRANK. Holy God!

ELLIS. Ha, ha! Wouldst toy at tierce and quatre with they rusting Spanish iron? Here's goodly English steel to whip thee home pell-mell! Ha and Ha! And ha!

FRANK (*Nervous*). Easy does it, sir!

The sound of bottles crashing from the dressing table.

ELLIS. That for thee and thy dancing-masters mincing roguery!

FRANK. Mind the mirror, sir!

ELLIS. Mirror me no mirrors, loon! (*Pauses out of breath.*) Not bad, eh Frank?

FRANK. Very expressive, sir.

The sword is returned to its scabbard.

ELLIS. Wig! Splendid.

FRANK. You look grand, Mr Brandon . . .

ELLIS. I think I'll

The telephone rings.

ELLIS. I'll take it. (*Pause while receiver is lifted.*) Gas, Light and Coke Company. Who is this? Oh Vera. Have you disconnected it? Discon-

by the switch, dear. Switch! Then throw a glass of gin over it . . .
Unkind? Are you surprised? I've endured eleven months and four days
of excruciating torment . . . And, since you're handy, Vera, I must ask
you to vacate your flat. Yes, I mean to breed budgerigars in there.
Don't cry, it runs into the carpet. Goodbye, Vera, I have to go to work.

He replaces the telephone.

I've done it! Bitched for good and all! She'll never fly that
broomstick again. If she calls again leave the phone of the hook.

FRANK. Yes, sir.

ELLIS. And if my wife calls first . . . no, leave that to me. Shall a wrinkled
beldame come twixt Dorset Smallpiece and his awful lust?

FRANK. Is that a proper question, sir?

ELLIS. 'Nay by this hanger and these tripes. Od's cuts, my Lord, no
huckster's hedgrow lechery —'

There is a knock on the door. The door is opened. ELLIS *draws
his sword.*

Who enters rudely thus? Prenez thy guard and draw!

BETH (*screams*). Ellis!

ELLIS. Approach, my chitterling.

BETH. Five mins, Ellis.

ELLIS. Mins?

BETH. Beginners on stage. Did you — um — look at Aubrey's suggestions?

ELLIS. I gave them the most cursory of glances.

BETH. Yes?

ELLIS. I refuse to consider the matter. In fact you can take this script
back to Mr Schwarz and you can invite him from me to impale
himself on it.

BETH. That scene's frightfully ripe, Ellis.

ELLIS. So, my love, is life. Frank, hat me.

BETH. Well, couldn't you glide over the more suggestive bits?

ELLIS. Glide, girl? What am I: a trombone?

BETH. You tend to relish the gamier bits, Ellis.

ELLIS. You're an experienced judge of vocal style, are you?

BETH. Of course I'm not.

ELLIS. Then leave well alone.

FRANK. The wig's not straight, sir.

ELLIS. Then straighten it, man. (*Pause.*) Tell me, how old are you, Miss Smithson?

BETH. Why do you need to know that?

ELLIS. Given luck, time, and a more varigated experience you may eventually own this theatre. When that moment arrives I'll defer to you in matters of delivery and everything else. In the meantime you must resist the urge to instruct me in my craft.

BETH. Cor!

ELLIS. Exactly.

The sword is returned to its scabbard.

ELLIS. Nosewipes, please, Frank. As for Aubrey's textual mutilations, I scorn them. He's no Doctor Johnson, is he? If he wants to push his point he'll have to take it up in person. I owe that much to the ghost of William Otterly. Now, you must excuse me. I have to goad a reaction from the paying cattle. How do I look, Frank?

FRANK. Done to a turn, Mr Brandon.

ELLIS. Yes, it's not half bad. I'll have the blue outfit tomorrow.

FRANK. I'll tell Mr William's dresser, sir.

ELLIS. No, Frank, you'll attend to it personally.

FRANK. But the funeral, sir!

ELLIS. Sorry, I need you here.

FRANK. Didn't you give me your word, Mr Brandon?

ELLIS. You extracted it under duress.

FRANK. What'll I do now?

ELLIS. I had a maiden-aunt just like your brother, Frank. I buried her regularly in Ascot Week for years on end. Good try, old fellow, but it didn't work. (*Pause.*) Are — are you engaged after this evening's revels, dear?

BETH. Yes, I am actually.

ELLIS. Oh. A romantic tie?

BETH. No. I'm going home to cut my corns.

ELLIS. Wouldn't you prefer to candlelit supper in amusing company?

BETH. Gosh, I would! But where could I find it at my age?

ELLIS. Humph! (*Pause. He resumes off.*) Watch me closely tonight, Miss Smithson. My antennae tell me you could witness great acting. My bow to you, Marm.

The door is closed.

BETH. Phew!

FRANK. Fantastic, isn't he?

BETH. Him? That feathered gas-bag?

FRANK. Half an hour ago he comes in here lookin' like two pennorth
o' catsmeat. Now he sails out like a golden galleon, his sails set and
all his guns bangin' away. You have to admire um.

BETH. Why? (*Pause.*) What was all that about a funeral?

FRANK. Aw, it's nothin'.

BETH. No, tell me, Frank.

FRANK. Me brother's bein' buried tomorrow. Mr B. says I could go,
then he changes his mind.

BETH. But of course you must go.

FRANK. I'd like to, Miss, only jobs are hard to come by.

BETH. So are brothers, I would have thought.

FRANK. Maybe I can work him round after the show. He's always up
after a good performance.

BETH. I could fix it in a minute.

FRANK. I wish you wouldn't, Miss.

BETH. Why ever not?

FRANK. It — it's the loyalty, isn't it?

Long pause.

BETH. You're potty. (*Pause.*) I have to make like a Stage Manager.

FRANK. Sure; you get away, Miss.

BETH. If you change your mind . . .

FRANK. I'll let you know.

*The door is opened and closed. After a pause we hear whiskey being
poured into a glass.*

FRANK (*sighs*). Here's to you, Stevey. I hope you're havin' better
weather — wherever you are (*He drinks slowly.*)

*After a moment, FRANK starts to walk around the room whistling
quietly to himself. He opens the window. The rain falls steadily, and
soon the splashing of it in the courtyard drowns all other sounds.*

SATURDAY NIGHT THEATRE

ATTARD
IN RETIREMENT

by John Peacock

To Jane Morgan

John Peacock was born in York in 1945 and educated in the Cotswold town of Stroud. He began writing in his early twenties and his first stage play *Children of the Wolf* transferred from the Dublin Theatre Festival to the Apollo in 1971. Since then he has worked mainly for film and television in this country and, briefly, in America.
Now living in Hertfordshire, he has spent the last two years writing for the theatre again. *Attard in Retirement* is his first play for radio.

Attard in Retirement was first broadcast on BBC Radio 4 on 7th April 1979. The cast was as follows:

WALTER ATTARD	George Cole
ARTHUR CRAWFIELD	Mark Dignam
ALICE CHAPMAN	Patricia Hayes
HILDA	Rosalie Crutchley
ERIC MAYBURY	John Gabriel
OLIVER HANWELL	Philip Voss
IAN	Philip Sully
TERRY FISHER	Peter Holt
MISS KIRK/BINGO ATTENDANT	Miriam Raymond
GARDENER (and other parts)	Michael Goldie
COMMISSIONAIRE (and other parts)	Alan Dudley
BANK TELLER	Peter Baldwin
CASHIER/RECEPTIONIST	Petra Davies
CALDER/KEN JONES	Eric Allan
DORIS/SARAH	Josie Kidd
BINGO CALLER/DRIVER	John Bull
IVY	Eva Stuart
WYN	Margot Boyd

Director: Jane Morgan

A hot summer's day. Hazy sounds of distant traffic, birdsong and children at play. Then, footsteps on a gravel path draw near to the sound of roses being pruned.

GARDENER. 'Morning, Mr Attard.

WALTER. Good morning. Beautiful rose. Masquerade.

GARDENER. Quite correct, Mr Attard.

The pace slackens. The sound of traffic grows.

WALTER (*softly and slowly*). Masquerade. Sea Pearl. My Choice. Emily Gray. Redgold. Elizabeth of Glamis. Peace.

Pause.

Ten out of ten, Mister Attard.

Music.

Well-spoken, assured business man. He sounds the car horn, muttering to himself.

OLIVER. Come on Eric. Blast you.

A car door opens. ERIC MAYBURY *gets inside, elderly, agitated and somewhat breathless. He is a nervous man.*

OLIVER. You just made it. He's leaving the park now.

ERIC. Thank goodness . . .

Car door closes.

OLIVER. Did you get the ledger?

ERIC. It wasn't there, Oliver. There's an accommodation agency on the first floor and Attard's office is above. All the post was in the entrance hall downstairs. A few circulars and that's all. No ledger.

OLIVER. When did you post it?

ERIC. Yesterday lunch. 12.30. It went first class.

OLIVER. What a waste of time all this is.

ERIC. What shall we do?

OLIVER. There's nothing we can do. You'll have to talk to Hilda . . . try and keep her calm.

Car starts up.

I must get to the Cheapside site. We're demolishing this afternoon. Are you coming with me . . . or what?

ERIC. Yes. Which is Attard?

OLIVER. Black crombie. Just going in now. Looks as if he's dressed for Winter. See him?

Car moves off.

ERIC. Oh . . . yes . . . yes . . .

OLIVER. Damn him . . .

Interior; slight echo of linoleum floored entrance hall and narrow staircase. Footsteps and rifling of envelopes as stairs are climbed.

WALTER. The Occupier . . . the occupier . . . so much waste-paper . . .

Door opens. A harsh elderly, pinched female voice, slices the air.

MISS KIRK. That you, Mr Attard?

WALTER. Oh, Miss Kirk . . . good morning.

MISS KIRK. How are we?

WALTER. Very well.

MISS KIRK. Nice weather for you.

WALTER. Yes.

MISS KIRK. The postman left this with the launderette. Too big for the letterbox you know.

Envelope changes hands.

WALTER. Thank you.

He moves upstairs.

MISS KIRK. Have a good day, then.

Door closes. WALTER's footsteps continue upstairs.

WALTER. Oh you miserable woman . . .

He pauses on the landing.

(*Sighs.*) My very own brass plate . . . 'Walter Attard'. Mustn't forget to take you.

He finds key and unlocks door. Enters office. Closes door. The warm, friendly voice of WYN FLETCHER.

WYN. I was beginning to think I'd come to the wrong office.

WALTER. Good heavens! I've just left you . . . I . . .

WYN. I rang for a mini-cab the moment you went out of the house. I decided that retiring after thirty-four years is not a thing a friend of mine should do alone.

WALTER. Oh Wyn . . .

WYN. You don't mind my being here, do you Walter?

WALTER. Treat . . . an especial treat.

WYN. I've made some coffee.

She moves into the kitchen.

WALTER. Oh if I'd known.

WYN. Well, you didn't. That was the point.

WALTER. I'd have done something. Look at this. Dust. I feel shamed that you should see my office looking like this.

Sound of crockery from kitchen.

WYN. Why on earth should you feel shamed?

WALTER. It's always been neat and clean and tidy.

WYN. So what? Don't be foolish.

WALTER. Spotless, whether anyone was expected or not. Until lately. It's just . . .

WYN *returns from kitchen with tray.*

WYN. For heaven's sake. We've known each other long enough. Those things don't matter.

WALTER. They do matter.

WYN. No . . .

WALTER. There should be pride. Right to the very end. There should be pride! By God, there was some pride thirty years ago. Spring in these feet in those days. I had my matric' under my belt and enough Yorkshire grit to sink a battleship. An office . . . in 1943, mark you, with its own lavatory and kitchen! What! My God, I meant to show the whole damned world.

Pause.

I was so sure in those days. So positive, Wyn. The future was as
certain to me as the past. Ah . . . and it was all going to be so . . .
grand! A huge finance house. 'Attard'! It's a good name. And it was
all here . . . in my head.

Pause.

Thus it started . . . thus it ended. But it was all here . . .

WYN. You've had a good business, Walter. Well respected.

WALTER. Sidelines. I always saw things from the sidelines. Can't get
away from it. The world was always waiting. But I never seemed to
step into it. No excitement.

WYN. Let's have this coffee, hmm?

WALTER. Yes . . .

He sighs, laughs at himself, ruefully.

Opening of envelope.

I've just let everything drift by. Taken no risks. I was never curious.
I've never grabbed hold of life. No excitement.

WYN. There's still time Walter. A lot can happen.

WALTER. I'm over sixty . . . retiring.

WYN. There's still time.

WALTER. Arthur Crawfield . . .! Well I'm blest.

WYN. What?

WALTER. This ledger . . . Arthur Crawfield . . . he was my first client.
The first and the last. I told him I was retiring. Unlike him to make
a mistake.

*Cut to empty, semi-demolished house, children playing in distance.
The harsh voice of sixty-three year old* HILDA STEWART.

HILDA. Attard sent us three letters and phoned us to say he was
retiring. Yet you still sent him the accounts for seventy-six.

ERIC. It was a mistake.

HILDA. Listen to him . . . a mistake! My God, you're damned right.

ERIC. I tried to get it back.

HILDA. And where is it?

ERIC. I told you, we . . .

OLIVER. Hilda . . . the demolition men will be here in five minutes to
explore the site. Eric and I are working. Please . . . will you leave
us . . . get back to the office . . . or go home. Do what you like . . .
but get rid of your paranoia elsewhere. It's driving me round the

bloody bend. Eric and I have tried to get the accounts back for you.
We've failed. Fini! You'll have to do what I said in the first place . . .
and wait till he sends the ledger back through the post. (*To* ERIC:)
Come on, lets go through here, we can see the whole site from
that window.

HILDA. If he sends it through the post!

Scrabbling over rubble.

OLIVER. Get this plank out of the way, Eric . . .

Plank thrust aside.

HILDA. Of course, *you're* not worried. Oh no!

OLIVER. That's right.

HILDA. But you went there!

OLIVER. That's right. An attempt to keep you quiet.

HILDA. Say what you like. Both of you. Rude as you want to be.
Take his side, Eric. Perhaps I look for things to go wrong too much
. . . but you . . . you don't even begin to be aware. We're co-directors
and I want to know . . . now . . . from both of you, what happens
if Walter decides to return those figures to Arthur in person?

OLIVER. What's the matter with you? Why should he? He's handled
those accounts since nineteen forty-four, and never been to Clay
Street since the war.

HILDA. Arthur was his first client, wasn't he? Now that he's retired
I think that he might return the ledger himself. A gesture.
Something to do. Re-acquaint with an old friend.

OLIVER. Oh do go away, Hilda. What if he does go round to Clay
Street. He will be returning a book, that's all. An accounts book in
perfect order. The man's not going to demand that Arthur be
dragged from his office waving his birth certificate. If he comes to
the office . . . if he asks to see Arthur . . . you say he's not in . . . you
says he's 'out'. All right?

ERIC (*gently*). Things do change, Hilda. I know that most people . . .

OLIVER. Just let her go home, Eric.

HILDA (*desperately, pitifully*). He must not come to Clay Street.

OLIVER. Relax.

HILDA. You're wrong. You're both very wrong . . .

ERIC (*tenderly, softly*). Come on, Hilda . . .

HILDA. . . . Very wrong . . .

Fade out.

Fade in. Interior. WALTER's *office. Silence. The click of a light switch up and down.*

WYN. The electricity's off now.

Pause.

Don't forget those books Walter.

Books picked up.

WALTER. Brontes. Been with me everywhere.

WYN. What are you going to do about that ledger?

WALTER. I don't know. I'm not sure yet . . .

Pause.

WYN (*gently*). Better go then.

Door opens. WYN *goes out.* WALTER *follows to doorway.*

WALTER (*very softly*). What a momentous occasion . . .

Door closes. A few bars of theme music which fade.

The sound of washing up. WALTER *finishing a meal.*

WYN. I thought you'd be lying in this morning. I was going to bring it up to you on a tray.

WALTER. You know me . . . up with the lark.

WYN. Where is it then . . . this firm?

WALTER. Clay Street. Tufnell Park.

Pause.

Just the two rooms . . . above a barber's shop.

WYN. Sounds like yours . . .

WALTER. Similar, yes. Very similar offices, except that his smelt of Brylcream. Whole place smacked of Brylcream . . . I remember that. The same size business as mine really. You can tell by the books. It's amazing what you can learn from people's accounts . . . how they live . . . the good years . . . and the bad. He was such a nice man, Wyn. A gentleman. Yorkshire too. He must be near retirement now. The same dreams . . .

WYN. Why haven't you seen him for such a long time?

WALTER. Well . . . I moved out here . . .

WYN. There are buses . . .

WALTER. It wasn't just that . . .

WYN. . . . and tube trains . . .

WALTER. There was one year . . . early on . . . when things seemed to be going really well . . . for him and for me. I nearly called him . . . but I didn't. You see the last true point of contact between us, the last thing we genuinely shared was our ambition . . . our plans and our dreams and what have you. As the years went by with none of them fulfilled, we felt let down, I suppose. Defeat. I understand and he understands, but it's difficult to explain.

WYN. Shall I take your plate?

WALTER. Through everything with Arthur and myself . . . five years . . . twenty . . . or fifty . . . or well, any number . . . there'll always be a bond. I will always know him . . . as I look in the mirror . . . as I hear myself think . . . as I put on my coat. Oh God, we planned such careers. We knew how badly each wanted success.

Pause.

Career's over. It seems to have gone by so quickly. In a flash. There always seemed plenty of time . . . and there wasn't.

Pause. He groans aloud.

WYN. Do you want any more coffee?

WALTER. No . . . no, thank you, Wyn . . .

Rises from table.

Get my coat on and be off.

Door opens. WALTER *goes into hall.*

Where's my scarf?

WYN. Mr Calder's leaving today. He's in the dining room. Did you add his bill up for me, Walter?

WALTER. On the sideboard.

WYN. Oh yes.

She joins WALTER *in the hall.*

Just be the two of us, then. Well, till the next lot, any way.

WALTER. Yes.

WYN. Come here. Look at that collar. That's better.

Door opens.

Ah Mr Calder.

CALDER. Lovely breakfast that, Mrs Fletcher.

WYN. Oh good. I'm glad you enjoyed it.

CALDER. Best there is and no mistake.

CALDER *starts to climb stairs.*

Not just a pretty face is she, eh Mr Attard?

WYN. Go on with you.

CALDER. I'll bring my cases down before I settle up the bill.

WYN. Right you are.

Door opens and closes upstairs. WYN *brushes* WALTER's *coat.*

WALTER. I do wish . . .

WYN *puts brush down.*

WYN. What Walter? What do you wish . . .?

Pause. WYN *speaks very tenderly.*

I've told you, Walter . . . it's no good wishing.

Fade out.

Heavy bustle. Crowds. Busy street in rush hour. The voice of a street vendor.

VENDOR. Lovely tomatoes here, lady . . . Clay Street? Yes, Guv'. There's no pub on the corner now though . . . left at the next traffic lights.

WALTER. Thank you . . . very much.

VENDOR. Thirty pence a pound. Who's going to have some of these . . .?

VENDOR's *voice starts to fade.* WALTER *moves towards Clay Street.*

Giving 'em away today, mum . . . honour of the Queen's birthday. Anybody else . . .?

WALTER *breathes heavily as he forges ahead.*

. . . now any more for any more . . .? How about you, lady . . .?

WALTER. Villier's Yard . . . that's right . . . It was the Villier's Arms . . . and this then . . . this must be . . . yes it is . . . Clay Street.

Clay Street is quieter as WALTER *turns into it.*

Must be halfway down . . . set back on the left . . . twenty-three . . .

Fade out.

Fade in. The street is quieter. WALTER's *footsteps.*

WALTER. The sweetshop . . . nineteen . . . twenty one . . . set back round here, should be . . .

Stunned silence.

. . . by gum.

Traffic passes.

By God . . .!

Car horn sounds irritably.

DRIVER. Get out of the way, you damned idiot!

WALTER. I . . . I . . .

DRIVER. What's the matter? Do you want to get yourself killed?

Car drives off.

WALTER. 'Crawfield . . . International . . . Enterprises' . . . By heck . . .!!

Cut to: Interior, large office reception hall. Soft music, cushioned sound.

COMMISSIONAIRE. Good morning, sir.

WALTER. Thank you. Yes . . . good morning.

COMMISSIONAIRE. Reception to your left, sir.

WALTER. Oh . . . thank you . . .

RECEPTIONIST. Good morning, sir. Can I help you?

WALTER. I wonder . . .?

RECEPTIONIST. Yes . . .?

WALTER. I was looking for . . . Arthur Crawfield Ltd.

RECEPTIONIST. Yes, that's one of our companies.

WALTER. I was hoping that I might see Mr Crawfield . . . if it's convenient. I have no appointment.

RECEPTIONIST. I'm sorry, there must be some mistake. There is no Arthur Crawfield.

WALTER. But . . .

Pause.

(*Laughs nervously.*) . . . No, I've been doing his accounts for years.

RECEPTIONIST. Arthur Crawfield Ltd . . . yes. It's just a name, though. There's no person.

WALTER. I once met him.

RECEPTIONIST (*calling to* COMMISSIONAIRE). There isn't an 'Arthur Crawfield' is there, Edgar?

COMMISSIONAIRE. I think so . . . at least there was . . .

RECEPTIONIST. Oh, I'm sorry . . .

COMMISSIONAIRE. He never comes in here though. I've never seen him and I've been doorman here for getting on . . . what . . . must be twenty years.

WALTER. It used to be a barber's shop. In the olden days.

COMMISSIONAIRE. Wouldn't know about that. What was it you wanted? Perhaps someone else can help.

WALTER. It's the accounts.

COMMISSIONAIRE. Well, if you'll take a seat over here, we'll see what the young lady can find out for you.

RECEPTIONIST. What's your name, sir?

WALTER. Attard. Walter Attard. Accountant.

As the RECEPTIONIST *dials a number* WALTER *and the* COMMISSIONAIRE *move away from her.*

Tell me . . . when was this building . . . built?

COMMISSIONAIRE. I should say early fifties, sir . . . late forties perhaps. Late forties, early fifties. Around then.

We hear the RECEPTIONIST *in the background.*

RECEPTIONIST. Yes. Jen. That's it. Accounts for Arthur Crawfield Ltd. I'll hang on.

WALTER. I haven't been here since the war. It was just two small rooms then . . . it's amazing . . . as I said . . . two small rooms above a barber's shop. It was owned by a widow . . . Emson. She used to clean the building as well . . . with her niece.

RECEPTIONIST. Yes, thanks, Fine. I'll tell him.

RECEPTIONIST *replaces telephone.*

WALTER. I can't believe it.

RECEPTIONIST. Mr Attard . . .

WALTER. Yes?

He returns to the desk.

RECEPTIONIST. I'm sorry, Mister Attard, I don't seem able to be of much help to you. These accounts are handled by Miss Stewart or Mr Hanwell and I'm afraid neither is available at the moment.

WALTER. I see.

RECEIPTIONIST. Do you want to leave the accounts with a message? I can see that they're passed on.

Pause.

It would be no trouble.

WALTER. That would be very kind of you. (*He hesitates.*) No . . . on second thoughts, I'll take this ledger with me. But thank you, all the same.

He starts to move away.

It's between Mr Crawfield and myself, you see. (*Pause.*) Old friends.

RECEPTIONIST. Very well. Goodbye, Mr Attard.

WALTER. Goodbye.

COMMISSIONAIRE. Have a good day, sir.

The RECEPTIONIST *starts to dial a number.*

WALTER. Thank you . . .

WALTER *leaves. Dialling continues.*

Cut to: Interior. Office. No musak. Telephone buzzing. Receiver picked up.

HILDA. Yes?

RECEPTIONIST (*telephone distort*). Reception here, Miss Stewart. Mr Attard's just left. I'm sorry but there wasn't much I could do. He's taken the ledger with him. He seemed determined to deliver it personally.

HILDA (*despairing*). He would be . . . Thank you. I'm leaving the office now. When Mr Maybury calls, tell him I'll see him at my home tonight.

RECEPTIONIST (*telephone distort*). Very good, Miss Stewart.

Telephone replaced. HILDA *sighs, muttering to herself.*

HILDA. What have we done . . .?

Fade out.

Fade in. Interior. HILDA's *drawing room. A clock chimes the quarter lightly and elegantly. The top is removed from a decanter.*

HILDA. Do you want ice with this or not, Eric?

ERIC. If it's there.

Ice in glass. Drinks poured during following.

HILDA. It was no mistake. (*Pause.*) Was it?

ERIC (*weakly*). What wasn't?

HILDA. Oh come on. Sending those accounts to Attard. You knew damn well what the consequences might be. Here . . . drink this.

ERIC. Thanks. It was a sudden thought . . . spur of the moment. I didn't mean to. Really. I regretted it instantly. Today . . . I wouldn't do it for the world. I just wanted someone to come along and find out the truth . . . to rid me of the responsibility. There's not a day goes by when something doesn't happen to stir the guilt . . . look at me . . . what good has it brought us. (*Pause.*) I couldn't help myself.

HILDA (*drily*). Poor Eric. Well maybe your ploy will pay off . . . and Attard rid you of your responsibility.

ERIC. I hope not. Truly.

HILDA. Truly isn't it a bit late to hope that.

ERIC. Oliver says he's not very bright.

HILDA. Yes, well by that he normally means the person's honest. Attard's adequate Eric and he did have ambition.

ERIC. You remember much about him?

HILDA. Not particularly. . . only that he flirted with me. He found me very attractive. I used to tease Arthur about it.

ERIC. Perhaps he still carries a torch.

HILDA. Oh God . . . it would have to be very heavily shaded. Anyway Eric . . . whatever you think of his capabilities as an accountant . . . he's a damn good sleuth.

ERIC. What do you mean?

HILDA. He's out there now . . . under the street lamp opposite. We're looking at each other. It didn't take him long to find Arthur's address did it?

ERIC. What are you going to do?

HILDA (*lighting a cigarette*). There's only one thing I can do. If he rings the doorbell I shall have to answer it. And if I let him in, I shan't want you here.

ERIC. Hilda, I just want to say . . .

Pause.

HILDA (*very softly, gently to* ERIC). I am capable of understanding the way you think, Eric . . . the way you feel. I can . . . and I do. The only difference is, as you know, I've found a way of coping.

Harsh front door bell.

It's out of our hands now. Disappear, through the library.

ERIC *leaves the room.* HILDA *goes through to the entrance hall.*

Here we go . . .

The front door opens.

WALTER. Good evening. Why . . . Miss Stewart. Hilda Stewart.

HILDA. I don't believe we've met.

WALTER. Yes. Attard. Walter Attard. In Arthur's old office. Above the barber's shop. We met once or twice. Walter Attard. Accountant.

HILDA. Oh yes . . . of course.

WALTER. I was calling on Arthur. I couldn't find his name listed in the telephone directory or I would have rung.

HILDA. You'd better come inside for a moment.

WALTER. Why . . . thank you.

Front door closes.

HILDA. Please . . . the drawing room.

WALTER. Thank you . . .

They enter the drawing room.

HILDA. Someone said you called in at the office this afternoon.

WALTER. Yes . . . Yes, I did.

HILDA. Giving director's addresses is against our policy. How did you find this one?

WALTER. I went to the Company Register Office. I didn't think that Arthur . . . Mr Crawfield would mind under the circumstances.

HILDA. You've put yourself to a lot of trouble.

WALTER. No, not really.

HILDA. Iniquitous. The company register. I think it's disgraceful that the address of any company director should be available so cheaply and so publicly. Still a shilling?

WALTER. Well . . . 5p.

HILDA. Yes . . . Anyway, I'm sorry, but I'm afraid I have to tell you that your second mission is useless. Arthur isn't here.

WALTER. Oh . . .

HILDA. Still . . . if you only wanted to return the book . . . That is why you came to the office this afternoon, isn't it? I can't think how it was sent out . . .

WALTER. That was the reason . . . but I really would like to deliver it personally now.

HILDA. What's the matter? The accounts are in order aren't they?

WALTER. Oh yes . . . yes . . .

HILDA. Well then . . .?

WALTER. Nothing like that. I must see Arthur.

HILDA. Why Mr Attard?

WALTER. I retired yesterday.

HILDA. Yes, I know.

WALTER. So one of my messages did get through. I thought no one had noticed my passing. The last thirty years have not been too successful for me, Miss Stewart. 'Well-thought-of' but that's about all. And I found some comfort, strange though it may seem, in believing Arthur's company had followed the same course. I visited Clay Street for consolation I suppose. I wanted the two of us to talk about the time in between. Thirty years is a long time. We had so many things we could talk about, I thought. Reasons for failure . . . about people being more important than business success. (*Pause. He continues quieter . . . a gentle frustration.*) That's what I went to Clay Street for . . . and then I saw the building. Well . . . such a grand place. Such a success. Oh . . . I wanted to . . . to rejoice in it with him. Today in Clay Street I saw everything Arthur and I had talked about thirty years ago. I saw everything I have ever wanted to be part of in my whole life! (*Simply, quite forlornly.*) I've got to see Arthur. I must know why he couldn't take me along with him . . . why he only allowed me to continue handling the smallest subsidiary of his business.

HILDA *is moved and upset by this.*

HILDA. I've told you, Mr Attard. Arthur isn't at home.

WALTER. But he does live here?

Pause.

When will he be back?

HILDA. He's changed considerably since you knew him. He sees nobody. He has an office in Clay Street but is never there. He won't see you. I know. That's it. I'm sorry.

WALTER. Do you know why Arthur Crawfield Limited was run as a totally separate company? It's as though I was 'kept out'.

Pause.

Do all the other subsidiaries have the same accountant?

HILDA. I believe so.

WALTER. Well, do they?

HILDA. Yes. They do.

WALTER. Why couldn't that accountant have been me?

HILDA. Perhaps Arthur thought you were not capable of such a position, Mr Attard.

WALTER. Oh no, no, no, no. I may look so now to you. In fact I probably am now . . . but not then. Oh no. Besides I trusted him implicitly . . . as he did me.

HILDA. Then you must put Arthur down in your book as a 'misplaced trust'. There can be no other reason.

WALTER. I can't believe that. I simply can't. When will he be back?

Front door is opened and closed.

Is that . . .?

IAN STEWART, HILDA's *thirty three year old son enters the drawing room.*

HILDA. Oh Ian . . . this is Mr Attard, an accountant. Mr Attard, my son . . . Ian.

WALTER. Pleased to meet you.

IAN. How do you do, Mr Attard.

HILDA. Mr Attard was just leaving.

IAN. I'll show you to the door.

HILDA. Will you be leaving the accounts book with me?

WALTER *speaks from the hall.*

WALTER. I wouldn't lie easy I'm afraid. It's a matter of pride, Miss Stewart. Good night.

The front door opens and closes.

Fade in. Interior WYN's *kitchen.*

WYN. But things do change, Walter. And people. That's life.

WALTER. No. You don't understand.

WYN. Forget it, Walter. You've retired.

WALTER. I can't 'forget it'. I don't know what, but something's wrong.

WYN. The books are in order.

WALTER. Yes.

WYN. Well then . . . that's all that matters.

Pause. WYN *changes to subject.*

Miss Kirk rang. She said your rubbish is blocking up the hallway and it's putting her clients off.

WALTER. 'Rubbish' . . . all my papers. And what are her clients . . .? A lot of squatters and tramps.

WYN. Walter . . .

WALTER. I'll see to it tomorrow.

Pause. WYN *is nervous. She is about to spring a surprise on* WALTER *and is tentative.*

WYN. The meal's ready.

WALTER. The meal . . .?

WYN. Yes.

Pause.

We're not eating in the kitchen tonight, Walter.

WALTER. Oh . . .?

WYN. Didn't you notice anything when you came in?

WALTER. No.

WYN. Nothing at all?

WALTER. Oh Lord, what on earth is it? Whatever's the matter?

WYN. Nothing. Nothing's the matter. Come here.

She crosses to the hallway.

We're eating in the dining room proper tonight.

WALTER *joins her.*

WALTER. With the guests . . .?

WYN. There are no guests. Mr Calder was the last one. You see, Walter, I've decided to retire too.

Pause.

Let's go in.

Door opens. Gentle, homely ticking of dining room clock.

WALTER. Good heavens . . .

WYN. I'll close the curtains. Quite dark outside.

Curtains are closed.

WYN. Don't stand in the doorway, Walter.

WALTER *enters room. Door closes.*

The food's all ready.

WALTER. No more guests, then . . .

WYN. That's why I asked if you'd noticed anything as you came in. The board's gone.

WALTER. No more guests.

WYN. No. I've taken the board down.

WALTER. What about me, Wyn? I'm a guest.

WYN. That's up to you. I . . . well, I'd like you to stay on here, of course.

WALTER. What do you think people would say . . .?

WYN. Oh . . . no more than they've been saying for the last twenty years since Clifford died. Sit down.

WALTER (*sitting down*). Yes . . .

WYN. Could you open that bottle for us.

WALTER. Wine . . .?

WYN. It's sort of . . . special . . . isn't it?

WALTER. Yes.

WALTER starts to open bottle.

WYN. Whatever people say it's sticks and stones now. Water off a duck's back. We're too old to care about what folk say, aren't we Walter?

Soup is ladled.

Besides I'm too fond of you to part. Some soup. Twenty years is a long time.

More soup ladled.

A life time.

Wine cork pops.

WALTER. There

He pours two glasses.

Looks a nice wine.

Pause.

WYN. Recommended. Highly . . . by the man in the shop.

WALTER drinks. Then he speaks, with great affection.

WALTER. Goes down grand.

WYN. Well, think about it.

Pause. She sits down.

Happiness, Walter.

Glasses clink.

WALTER. Happiness.

Cut to: Interior. HILDA's *drawing room. Loud knocking on door.*

Handle being sharply turned back and forth.

HILDA. Go away. Will you go away. Once and for all will you go away . . .

IAN (*beyond door*). Oliver's here.

HILDA. What for? I didn't invite him.

IAN (*beyond door*). Well he's here, so you might as well . . .

HILDA. I might as well . . . nothing! If he's here when I didn't call him . . . then he can sod off.

OLIVER (*beyond door*). It's me Hilda. Let me in.

HILDA. You're not deaf. You heard what I said. Do it.

OLIVER. Please, Hilda. Let us in.

HILDA. No.

OLIVER (*beyond door*). I shall call the police.

HILDA (*laughing bitterly*). Oh my God, will you? and have your co-director up on a drugs charge. I think not.

She is now close to the door.

OLIVER (*beyond door*). Come on, Hilda . . .

IAN (*beyond door*). Mother, I want to help. For my sake . . . just for me . . . please will you open this door. (*Pause.*) Mother I can't bear it.

After a pause the key is turned in the lock, OLIVER *and* IAN *enter.*

OLIVER. Thank you.

HILDA. I didn't open it for you. This is my private room. I didn't ask you here. You're as welcome here as I am in your site office. We're business partners, Oliver. To you . . . my private door is always locked

OLIVER. I was sent for, so I came.

HILDA. He had no business to ask you.

OLIVER. We're worried about you.

HILDA. Don't play charm boy, Oliver. God spare us that little performance. You couldn't give a damn about me or my necrotic nostrils. As far as you're concerned I can go to blazes. Right? Am I right? Yes, you bet I am right! Yes . . . let us get the facts straight!!

Don't touch me! I don't like being touched!! (*Pause.*) The business. That's all you care about. 'S all you've ever cared about . . . and Eric creeps after you like the crawler that he is. You're afraid I'll talk to Attard and louse up the business. You think this will make me talk? . . . Wrong! Listen . . . booze makes me throw up. Cocaine gets me through the day . . . each day . . . without much anguish . . . Do you hear . . . without much anguish to myself . . . and very little to anybody else . . . well . . . NONE to anybody else. . . (*Pause.*) Do you understand that? Right? Right!! Alrrrrrright . . . then disappear, will you. (*Pause.*) Oh go on for God's sake!

OLIVER. Where is it?

IAN. On her desk . . . inside that cigarette box.

HILDA (*wearily*). Don't bother yourself. I'll only get more.

OLIVER. Leave it, Ian.

HILDA. Ah . . .! Thank you sirrrrrrr. I promise you this, Oliver . . . on cocaine my mouth is shut . . . on cocaine I don't need to talk. I'll keep our secret . . .

She lurches to OLIVER *and whispers savagely in his ear.*

. . . and in particular . . . yours.

OLIVER. I don't know what you're talking about.

HILDA (*loudly, flatly*). Leave me alone will you. Piss off the pair of you.

OLIVER. I'll see myself out.

He leaves the drawing room. HILDA *shouts after him.*

HILDA. Why not . . . you saw yourself in, didn't you?!

The front door opens and closes

Pause.

All right, Ian. Don't say anything. Don't . . . say . . . any . . . thing. Please. Don't reproach. Nothing.

Silence. Then gradually, we become aware of HILDA *crying. The crying turns into sobs, uncontrollable weeping.*

IAN. Don't . . . Mother . . .

HILDA. I'm tired of it all . . . I want out. I want so much to get out.

IAN. Don't . . . please don't . . .

HILDA. It was all for you . . . I went along with it all for you. I betrayed Arthur . . . everything we ever lived for . . . I betrayed. I must not let it be all for nothing. Walter Attard cannot find out. He cannot. He cannot . . .

IAN. . . . ssh . . .

HILDA. He . . . must not . . . look . . . for Arthur . . .

Fade out on HILDA's *sobs as* IAN *comforts her.*

Interior. Newsagent's shop.

NEWSAGENT. Craven A. He used to come in here every morning for ten Craven A. Thin fellow. Glasses. Building business. Am I right?

WALTER. Go on.

NEWSAGENT. Let me see. We're talking about a long time ago, you know. Can't have seen him since . . . (*Whistles.*) . . . Oh must have been the end of the war. Still deliver the papers there. Times, then. Telegraph now. His young lady . . . well young lady as was still lives there.

WALTER. 'Still' lives there? You mean 'Hilda Stewart'.

NEWSAGENT. Yes. With her son.

WALTER. Has she always lived there?

NEWSAGENT. Oh yes . . . they were always, you know . . . like that. She'll know where he is if anybody does.

WALTER. I see . . . thank you. But you haven't seen him since the war.

NEWSAGENT. I used to wonder where he was . . . and then you don't, do you? Stops crossing your mind. No, if I'm going to be honest . . . I thought he was dead.

Romantic radio music. Telephone ringing. Washing up in foreground.

WYN. Every blessed time I put my hands in water . . .

Radio is turned down. Telephone picked up.

Hello. Wyn Fletcher speaking. (*Silence.*) Hello. This is Wyn Fletcher speaking. Is anybody there . . .?

Caller replaces their receiver. Dialling tone. WYN replaces hers.

Oh dear . . .

She turns the radio off altogether.

I hate those . . .

Clock ticks. Music fades.

Cut to: Interior. Reception hall of Crawfield International. Musak as before with distant vacuum cleaner.

WALTER. This is all fourteen subsidiary companies of Crawfield International?

RECEPTIONIST. That's right.

WALTER. You don't mind if I take this list, do you?

RECEPTIONIST. Well, no . . . I suppose . . .

WALTER (*reading*). Crawfield London. A.C.D. Crawfield Ceramics . . .

RECEPTIONIST. Here's Miss Stewart now.

HILDA, ERIC and OLIVER *approach.*

WALTER. Ah . . . Miss Stewart . . . Mr Maybury . . . Mr Hanwell . . . the triumvirate.

HILDA. This is Mr Attard. Do you remember him Eric? Oliver?

ERIC. Ah yes . . . Walter Attard.

WALTER. If Arthur was here we'd have a full old time board meeting.

OLIVER. A real barber's shop quartet . . . hmm, Walter?

WALTER. Yes . . .

HILDA. I told you Arthur wouldn't be in today.

WALTER. Yes. I came to see the young lady at the desk.

OLIVER. So, there's nothing we can do for you, Walter?

WALTER. Thank you . . . no

RECEPTIONIST. Maybe Miss Stewart could help you, Mr Attard.

WALTER. Oh I don't think so.

HILDA. Not unless you ask at any rate.

RECEPTIONIST. Mr Attard was wondering . . .

WALTER. I was wondering if anyone knew the address of the cleaner . . . Edith Emson who owned the barber's shop. That's all. She had a niece . . . Alice somebody . . . No importance.

Silence.

ERIC. I . . . I can't recall . . .

WALTER. No matter. Someone in the district should know.

HILDA. Is that what brought you into town?

WALTER. Partly . . . not mainly . . . and why not? Here's your son, Miss Stewart. You see . . . I'm a gentleman of leisure now . . . I can go where my fancy takes me. Excuse me.

He goes to the main door.

Good morning, Ian.

IAN. Mr Attard.

WALTER (*warmly, expansively*). Good day all . . .

He leaves.

HILDA. Follow him, will you, Ian?

IAN. What . . .? Why in God's . . .

HILDA. Please. I want you to follow him. I'll replace you as soon as I can with someone else.

OLIVER. Hilda . . . don't be ridiculous . . .

HILDA. Ian.

IAN. All right, mother . . . whatever you say.

He leaves.

ERIC. Alice Chapman . . . Do you think he'll find her?

HILDA. Yes.

Interior Top Rank bingo hall. The bingo caller is always distorted through a microphone.

CALLER (*distort*). There you are. Give the lady her card, my little darling and we're all set for full house on the green page. While that's happening I'd just like to tell you that Harry your manager and friend, Happy Harry, is improving in St. Mary's and should be back with us some time next week.

We follow WALTER in the foreground.

WALTER. Could I have a book, please?

WOMAN ATTENDANT. I don't see why not, dear. Mind, we're halfway through, you know . . . only one more game up to the interval.

WALTER. Oh, I see.

ATTENDANT. Just the one book, is it sir?

WALTER. Oh yes please. Just the one.

ATTENDANT. That's 40p.

WALTER. Thank you.

CALLER. In the meantime, any problems you have, bring 'em all here to yours truly. Mike Johnson. All right, are you, darling? You can bring your problems round any time. Book back now, is it, dear?

WALTER. There we are . . . forty pence.

CALLER. Can't hear you? Got it? Has the last winner got her book back, Patsy?

PATSY. Yes!

WALTER. Look . . . a friend of mine is here . . . a lady called Alice Chapman. I'm told she's wearing a blue coat. Would you know her?

ATTENDANT. No, dear.

WALTER. About fifty . . .

ATTENDANT. I've only been here a week. Try the evening game. Somebody there might help you.

CALLER. Now we'll wait till the gentleman's ready and we're off . . .

Pause.

Are you ready sir?

ATTENDANT. They're waiting for you.

WALTER. Oh . . .

CALLER. In the black coat, sir. Ready sir?

WALTER. Yes . . . I'm sorry.

CALLER. Right you are. Get my balls back in circulation. Whoops, naughty! And we're all set. Eyes down. Green page for the last game before the interval, and this is for full house. Full house only. For seventy-eight pounds and forty pence . . . Three and four. Thirty-four.

WALTER. Good gracious . . . so many Alice Chapmans . . . which is you . . .?

CALLER. All the twos . . . twenty-two. One and four . . . fourteen. On its own . . . number eight . . .

Fade out.

Fade in. Rapid pips of telephone kiosk. Coin inserted. Background traffic.

IAN. Hello Mother, I'm outside the Bingo Club on the Holloway Road. We came here straight from the sweet shop on the corner of Clay Street.

HILDA (*distort*). Stay there. There'll be somebody to take your place soon. Terry Fisher. I've told him what you're wearing.

IAN. I hope he's quick. How do I get back?

HILDA. I'll send the Rover to pick you up.

IAN. Thank you.

IAN *sighs. Fade out.*

Fade in. Bingo hall. The game proceeds.

CALLER. Six and three . . . sixty-three. Four and seven . . . forty-seven. Two fat ladies . . . eighty-eight. On its own . . . Number nine.

WALTER (*thoughts*). Too old . . . what about . . . mmm . . . mmm . . . (*sighs.*) . . . what about . . .

CALLER. Legs . . . Eleven.

WALTER (*thoughts*). Yes . . . Alice Chapman . . . I think that's you . . .

CALLER. Five and one . . . Fifty-one.

MAN PLAYER. Bingo!

People move and chatter as we start to home in on the voice of ALICE CHAPMAN.

WALTER. I think that's you . . .

ALICE. I'm going to get my winnings on the first game Ivy. Up to the office.

IVY. O.K. love. Do you want anything?

ALICE. Tea, will you dear, and a packet of crisps.

She moves towards door.

Cheese and onion. Smokey bacon if not.

Cut to: Marble floored foyer. Faint noise of auditorium.

DORIS. Never again have you Alice?!

ALICE. Only a line. Ten quid.

DORIS. Better than a poke in the eye.

ALICE. Have you won?

DORIS. No . . . ladies.

ALICE starts to climb stairs.

WALTER. Alice Chapman?

ALICE. Yes.

Pause.

I don't know from where, but I know that face.

WALTER. Attard. Walter Attard.

ALICE. Good Lord, so it is. My . . . fancy seeing you after all this time. What a gent, eh?

WALTER. You were so big . . .

ALICE. Christ . . . come off it! But thanks. God, I can't get over it, Clay Street seems a long way away now, doesn't it eh? What you doing in here?

WALTER. Looking for you.

ALICE. Me? Go on with you . . . I'm sure you've better folk to see.

Pause.

Come on. What are you doing?

WALTER. I've come to see you.

ALICE. How did you know where I was?

WALTER. I found out from the grocer on the corner of Clay Street.

ALICE. Wally's boy.

WALTER. Wally Jones.

ALICE. That's right. Him as had the barber's shop. He's been good to me, he has.

WALTER. He wouldn't give me your address, naturally, not really knowing me . . .

ALICE. No . . .

WALTER. . . . but he lent me his club membership card to here and said this is where I might find you.

ALICE. Well, well . . .

WALTER. He said you'd moved to a place with your Aunt Edith years ago.

ALICE. That's true. Dead now though. God bless her. A year this Christmas gone. Good age, you know. Nearly eighty-eight she was. There's a lot die younger.

WALTER' I'm sorry.

ALICE. Yes . . . anyway . . . can't all be roses . . .

WALTER. Must be lonely for you now.

ALICE. Lonely? Not really. I'm on my own nowadays, it's true, but I wouldn't say lonely, no. Spend most of my time here . . . and then . . . I get the odd good looking accountant popping in to see me. Have to get my hair done if this keeps up.

Pause. Then quite practically.

What did you want me for, love?

WALTER. I'm trying to find Arthur Crawfield.

Pause.

ALICE. That's a name to conjure with. You don't still work for him, then?

WALTER. Sort of.

ALICE. Whatever that means. Haven't seen him anyway. Not that I would really . . . once the area was bombed we moved out of course. Lived in the methodist hall on the corner of Hill Street for a couple of weeks, but that's all. Mr Crawfield was running his business from a caravan type thing parked on the bomb site, but I never saw him again after that night.

WALTER. What night was that?

ALICE. What? The bombs?

WALTER. Yes. The last time you saw him.

ALICE. August the sixteenth, nineteen forty-four. A Wednesday. I'll never forget that night. I'd forget my own birthday first. Those buzz bombs. Count six and pray. The first bomb fell at a quarter to nine.

WALTER. Where was Crawfield?

ALICE. In his office. In a rare old state about something or other. He got me and Aunt Edith to witness a paper for him . . . a form thing. All legal looking. I'd never done it before, you know, put my name to anything, so naturally it was a big thing . . . not having done it before.

WALTER. What was it?

ALICE. I don't know. He'd got it folded over so we couldn't read it. 'Just sign there' he says . . . and 'put the date' . . . oh yes, we put the date as well. Then we left. Quick sharpish. Bloody bombs like snow and there we were . . . writing our names on bits of paper.

WALTER. You've no idea what it was?

ALICE. No . . . of course we laughed about spying and such . . . some people said he had sympathies with the Germans . . . God knows why, and I didn't believe it.

Pause.

We just laughed about it if you understand me.

WALTER. Was he in his office when you left?

ALICE. Oh yes.

WALTER. And you haven't seen him since?

ALICE. No . . . (*becomes slightly cagey, wary.*) Well, we settled in the East End after that.

Pause.

He's all right, isn't he?

WALTER. I haven't seen him.

ALICE. Oh . . . (*Pause.*) . . . not since then you mean?

WALTER. I've heard from him naturally.

ALICE. Of course.

Pause.

Even if you only work for him 'sort of' eh?

WALTER. Yes.

ALICE. There were several odd things about that night.

WALTER. What sort of things?

ALICE. Oh . . . things that might be of use to someone.

Pause.

Just get my winnings while there's no queue.

She crosses to pay out desk. WALTER *waits.*

CASHIER. Membership card and voucher, love.

ALICE. Here we are. That's them . . .

CASHIER. That's one, two, three, four, five, and one fiver.

ALICE. Thank you.

Returns to WALTER.

Ten pounds. Not bad, eh?

WALTER. No . . .

ALICE. You're not the first one to ask me questions about Arthur Crawfield, you know. Not by a long chalk.

Pause.

Look dear . . . you don't want to come in for the second half, do you? I'll tell you what. You go away for a bit and think about things. We'll be finished here by four. Come back, then, and if you can find your way to make it worth my while, I'll tell you all I know about that night.

WALTER. Oh Alice Chapman, I don't know about . . .

ALICE (*descending stairs*). They'll be starting in a minute. Four o'clock in here.

WALTER. The membership card. You're to give it back to Jones for me . . .

ALICE (*some distance away*). Give it me later. Four o'clock.

WALTER *sighs.*

Cut to: Telephone booth. Traffic back-ground. Rapid pips. Coin inserted.

IAN. Hello, mother. Terry whatever his name is didn't turn up at Holloway Road. I'm now at the Company Register Office in City Road. Have you got that?

Fade out.

Fade in. An office. Distant typewriting. Telephones.

REGISTRAR. Here we are. I've been through the records of all fourteen subsidiary companies and it appears that your Mr Arthur Crawfield is only on the board of one of them. That is . . . (*Rifling through papers.*) Arthur Crawfield Ltd. which was formed in 1942.

WALTER. But his name is on most of those subsidiary company titles.

REGISTRAR. Well, you can name a company anything you like. It doesn't have to be called after one of its directors.

WALTER. So Arthur Crawfield has had nothing whatsoever to do with the forming of any company since the war.

REGISTRAR. No, sir. All the directors are variations of Hilda Stewart, Oliver Hanwell, Eric Maybury and Ian Stewart.

WALTER. So . . . Ian Stewart . . . But no Arthur Crawfield since that first company of all.

REGISTRAT. That's right, sir.

Out to: Church clock strikes four. Outside bingo hall. An old car. Sounding as if it only just passed its M.O.T. pulls up at the kerb. The engine is still running as TERRY FISHER, *the driver, a young man in his early thirties, speaks to* IAN *at the kerb through the car window.*

TERRY. You Ian Stewart?

IAN. At last.

TERRY. Terry Fisher. Private Investigator. I've just got here from City Road. Telephone problem. Where's Attard?

IAN. He came straight here from the Company Register, went to the bank and he's over there now looking in that jeweller's . . . see him? Dark coat . . . hat.

TERRY. That's right . . . I've got him.

IAN. It seems he's going back into that Bingo Hall on the corner . . . yes, there he goes.

TERRY. Fine. I'll pull up and park. There's a chauffeur a couple of hundred yards back . . . with your Rover.

Fade out.

Interior. Bingo hall. Voices have slight echo in the empty cinema.

ALICE. There's nobody'll bother us . . . least not till I've said what you want to hear.

WALTER. The sixteenth of August . . .

ALICE. Edith and me went up there about eight. The place was in a terrible mess . . .

WALTER. Arthur's office . . .?

ALICE. Yes. There was going to be a board meeting the next day, or so he said . . . but the room was a right pig's hole, I'm telling you. Another funny thing . . . same time . . . about eight . . . a big blue car came up Clay Street . . . didn't see many coloured cars those days. They were all black; that's why it stuck out in my memory. Anyway it parked on the reccy . . . you know the waste ground alongside number fifteen, where the car park is now. It was still there when Aunt Edith and me went off to the shelter. By that time of course, we'd had the warnings and the buggers were dropping like nobody's business . . . but this car was still there . . . calm as you like . . . the driver just sitting . . .

WALTER. You didn't recognise him?

ALICE. Couldn't see, dear. Not for want of trying, mind you. But it was pouring down that night . . . couldn't see through the glass. Heavens hard. Cats and dogs.

WALTER. What happened to the paper that you signed?

ALICE. Mr Crawfield said he'd take it round to his bank. By hand. I offered to post it for him. But no . . . he said 'By hand'. It must have been very important.

WALTER. I see.

ALICE. I'm going to tell you something now, Mr Attard that I've never uttered to a living soul, but, since Aunt Edith's gone . . . I see no harm. That night she collected Crawfield's rent . . . and Wally Jones' . . . you know . . . the barber. He owed a month . . . five weeks, so it was quite a bit. She'd put the money in her bag to take with her as she didn't want to leave it in the flat . . . in case of looters and such-like. There was a lot of that went on during raids . . . especially round Tufnell Park. Anyway we'd reached the shelter, when she remembered she'd left the bag in Crawfield's office. Well, blow me, if she didn't get up and go back for it. That was the sort of person she was . . . once she'd made up her mind . . .! Anyway . . . off she went. She came back with the bag about twenty minutes later. She never said anything, but I knew something had happened . . . she was . . . how can I say . . . well just different . . . and she had a smear of blood on the back of her hand . . . she said she'd caught it on some-thing . . . but there was no cut there. She wouldn't talk about the blue car . . . or Crawfield . . . or anything . . . just refused even to mention it . . . his name . . . the car . . . if she'd seen him again . . . anything . . . but . . . and this is the important thing, Mr Attard . . . do you know that from that Wednesday until the day she died . . . she got a postal order for ten pounds on the last Thursday of every single month. (*Pause.*) I know. I lived with her. I saw them.

WALTER. She never said who they were from?

ALICE. No . . . (*Pause.*) . . . but I looked at one once, and I know the name of the issuing Post Office.

Pause.

Fifty quid.

WALTER (*sighing*). Really . . . I . . .

ALICE. Course if it's not important to you . . .

WALTER. Do you know which bank Arthur Crawfield was going to take that document to? The one you signed . . .?

ALICE. That and the Post Office which issued the postal orders for fifty quid . . . and the bank wasn't the same as saw to his business.

WALTER. Oh . . . Alice . . .

ALICE. Come on, what's it to you? People pay more for dafter things. I need a new coat. Look at this rag. Winter's coming on an' all.

WALTER. I've already given you enough for a winter coat.

ALICE. Well . . . (*Pause.*) . . . Forty.

WALTER. Forty. In here. Tomorrow afternoon.

ALICE. It's a deal. God bless you, Mr Attard.

WALTER *rises and starts to leave.*

WALTER. Alice . . . you said I wasn't the first person to ask you questions about Mr Crawfield . . . Who was?

ALICE. One of his co-directors . . . Hilda Stewart.

WALTER. Hilda Stewart . . .?

ALICE. Tomorrow. Fourish.

Fade out.

Fade in. The rapid pips of a telephone call box. Coin inserted. The booth is inside a building.

ALICE. Alice Chapman here. Edith Emson's niece.

Pause.

That's right. I thought you'd remember. I wrote to tell you she'd died. We were very close Edie and I. I've been offered seventy-five quid for information about Arthur Crawfield and what happened on a certain night in August, 1944.

Pause.

I mentioned postal orders . . . but that's all. What I say next is up to you. I'm being paid another visit tomorrow, if you want me to put him off the scent, then you'd somehow better see me tonight . . . perhaps we could come to some arrangement . . . like you had with Edie . . . mind . . . times have changed . . . what with inflation and all . . . I'll tell you where I'll be . . .

Fade out.

Fade in. The infernal clanging of a refuse disposal lorry. WALTER, panting and shouting rushes towards it.

WALTER. No . . .! Wait! Leave them!! Hey!!

DUSTMAN. What . . .???

WALTER. Please . . . those papers . . . leave them would you?

DUSTMAN. Stroll on, mate, we've been sent special to pick this lot up.

WALTER. I'm sorry . . . I do apologise . . . I'm sorry . . . it's a mistake . . . please would you . . . please leave them . . . inside . . . just in the hallway.

DUSTMAN. All right guv.

Cut to: Hallway as bundles are dumped.

WALTER. Thank you.

MISS KIRK. Mr Attard . . .!

DUSTMAN. If you want 'em . . .

WALTER. Yes. Good day.

Door closes. Shutting out street sounds. WALTER *gathers his breath.*

MISS KIRK. It's not good enough, Mr Attard. This is no smiling matter. I sent for those men myself at no small inconvenience.

WALTER. I'm sorry . . . I'm truly sorry, Miss Kirk. I didn't mean to smile, but I needed these papers. Now my telephone upstairs is no longer connected. Do you think you could call a taxi cab for me and I'll take these back to Mrs Fletcher's.

MISS KIRK. You'll need a van. You won't get all those in a taxi.

WALTER. The ones I want, Miss Kirk . . . the ones I want . . .

Cut to: Interior. WYN's *kitchen. The rustle of papers.*

WYN. Here's a signature, Walter. July the . . . twelfth it looks like . . . 1944.

WALTER. Let me see . . . 'Arthur Crawfield'.

WYN. Here's another . . . July the twenty-seventh . . .

WALTER. 'Arthur Crawfield' . . .

WYN. . . . . September the eleventh.

WALTER. Yes. Give me that. Eric Maybury . . . P.P. Arthur Crawfield . . . in his absence.

WYN. What's P.P.?

WALTER. Per Pro . . . By Proxy. Is there a document in between . . . after the sixteenth of August.

WYN. Yes . . . there's a copy of a contract signed on the seventeenth of August.

WALTER. Atherton . . . I remember that . . . contract for a chemical factory. Arthur wasn't too keen if I remember . . . seventeenth . . .

the day after the bombing. (*Sighs heavily.*) 'Arthur Crawfield'. . .
well, the signature's there. Let's compare it with an earlier one . . .

WYN. Here . . .

WALTER. That will do . . .

WYN. Is it good or bad, Walter?

WALTER. Well, one thing's for sure, Wyn . . . these signatures are
different.

Pause. Breathless excitement.

By God . . . they're different!!

Cut to: HILDA's *drawing room.*

IAN. You've never allowed me to see any books or any papers
connected with Arthur Crawfield Ltd. Any other company bar
that. Why?

HILDA (*slurred*). Go away . . . please . . . you're boring . . .

IAN. Come on, mother, this is bloody serious. I'm not a flaming child.
Whatever's going on . . . Whatever Attard might stumble across . . .
it's to do with those books, isn't it? And it must be serious . . .
look at you . . . what it's doing to you.

HILDA (*laughs wearily*). Yeh . . . look . . .

IAN. I can go to Oliver or Eric, but I'd rather you told me. Where is
my father?

HILDA. Where do you think he is? Huh?

IAN. I've no idea.

HILDA. Think. Why do you think I've never been able to tell you . . .

IAN. Is he dead?

HILDA. Yes . . .

Pause. HILDA *lights a cigarette.*

For God's sake . . . rest his soul . . . yes. Well, you can go now. That's
it . . . Don't tell any . . . well . . . sod it, eh . . .

IAN. When did he die?

HILDA. Oh . . . before your time . . . just . . . just . . . a month or so
before your time . . .

IAN. And Attard doesn't know he's dead?

HILDA. No . . .

IAN. And is that what you don't want him to find out?

HILDA. Why we covered up . . . and why he had to die.

IAN. 'Why' he had to die?

Pause.

What do you mean 'Why' he had to die?

HILDA. . . . oh . . . don't . . . I don't know . . . go . . .

IAN. What are you saying? Are you saying that he was murdered?

HILDA. Am I saying that at last?

Pause.

Absolutely.

IAN. By who . . .?

Cut to. Interior public house. Bar noise.

ALICE. What do you think then?

IVY. I think it's terrific. Must have knocked you back a bob or two.

ALICE. Nice red . . .

IVY. I like the colour.

ALICE. Courtesy of a gentleman friend. Keep me warm in winter, he said. Nice man. Cheers me up. 'S really cheered me up to have something new, Ivy. Can't remember when I last had something new.

IVY. Who's the postcard for?

ALICE. This? For 'im. Do him a turn. Well, I feel like it. I feel all good . . .

IVY. You've missed the last post now.

ALICE. Have I? Well, if I have . . . it'll go tomorrow. same again, Vic . . .

Fade out as glass is put on bar.

Fade in. WYN's kitchen.

WALTER. Arthur never signed a document after the twenty-seventh of July 1944.

WYN. Oh . . . Walter . . .

WALTER. No . . . it's true. Every one of those signatures is a forgery. There's no trace of Arthur since August the sixteenth 1944.

WYN. So where is he?

WALTER. I think he's dead Wyn . . .

WYN. That's a dreadful thing to say.

WALTER. I know it is.

Pause.

I shall soon find out. I'm nearly there. Alice will help me.

WYN. Who's Alice?

WALTER (*wickedly*). An old flame.

WYN. Don't joke about it. I worry.

WALTER. You mustn't.

WYN. But I do. If you think something that fishy's going on why don't you call the police.

WALTER. Because it's my adventure! Don't you see that, Wyn? All right . . .! Arthur may have hurt his hand in the raid and so his signature altered . . . he may not want to see me . . . he might have thought me inadequate to carry the firm's business, and just given me that first account for luck . . . and I may be just being foolish . . . but God, I'd forgotten what it was like to get up in the morning because I wanted to do something . . . to wonder what the end of the day will bring! I feel like a young man again. The last twenty years . . . my God! What did I do in them?

WYN. It was always tomorrow with you. The next and the next. Still is if I know my Mr Attard.

WALTER. No . . . not any more. Come here, will you.

WYN. What?

WALTER. Come on. Come over here a bit, will you? Let me put my arm around you.

He does so.

WYN (*fondly*). You're a fool.

WALTER (*softly, gently*). Eh?

Pause.

Dance with me, Wyn.

WYN. Walter . . .

WALTER. May I have the pleasure of this dance?

WYN. But there's no . . .

WALTER. Ssssh . . . tonight there is . . .

WYN *laughs gently as they waltz.*

Cut to: Bingo hall.

CALLER. I hear that both our link-up clubs are packed out tonight, ladies and gentlemen, so you can expect a big full house prize of around five hundred pounds . . . but that's not till the game after next . . .

ALICE. Got the time, Ivy?

IVY. I make it just coming up to nine.

ALICE. I've got to nip out for a minute.

IVY. Where you off then?

ALICE. See a man about a dog. Only in the yard. Keep an eye on my coat, there's a love.

CALLER. Lots of fun and games to be had before then . . . and you're having it, aren't you Mrs. Put that man down, I say. I say 'put that man down' . . . you wicked girl . . .

ALICE has stood up and we now go outside with her. The caller is just audible from inside the hall. Faint traffic. A cat mews and scurries off.

Are we ready Patsy, love? Can I go? Not yet. I can't. The winner of the next game by the way . . . two hundred cigarettes for the one line . . . four hundred for the full house . . .

ALICE. Come on . . . where are you . . .?

Cat mews.

Hello, puss . . .

Pause.

. . . Brrrr . . . it's nippy. Wish I'd kept my coat on . . .

Cut to: Interior. WYN's kitchen.

WALTER. Put your glass down.

WYN. What?

WALTER. Put your glass down. The young don't have the prerogative in permissiveness, you know, Wyn.

Pause.

I want to kiss you.

They kiss tenderly.

WYN. Oh Walter.

Cut to: Yard behind bingo hall. Caller's voice continues dimly. The church clock is striking nine.

ALICE. Either that clock's fast or Ivy's watch is slow. Don't know which, do you Tabby, eh?

CALLER. Can I go? I can go! I can hear you all panting now. Eyes down. I want eyes down now for line one on the pink page . . . Seven and three . . . seventy-three. Six and eight . . . sixty-eight. On it's own . . . number six. Kelly's eye . . . number one . . .

ALICE. Here's a car. You'd better skedaddle . . .

The cat mews.

. . . go on.

*The cat mews and scuttles away. A car approaches. The car stops
but the engine keeps ticking over.*

Hello . . .?

No reply.

Are you looking for me? . . . Alice . . . Alice Chapman.

She approaches the car.

I thought it was you . . .

*The car suddenly accelerates, lurches forward and mows ALICE
down. She falls to the ground. We stay with her.*

No . . . no . . . oh please dear God . . . no . . .

*The car reverses. Screeches backwards, then lurches forward again.
Then reverses.*

I can't move . . . oh no . . . this is it . . . oh God . . . sweet God . . .
bless me . . . forgive me my s. . .

*The car screams forward over ALICE, then reverses. Then goes
away . . . The silence is unbearable. The cat mews and faintly we hear.*

CALLER. On its own . . . number eight. Two and three . . . twenty-three.
All the fours . . . forty-four . . .

The sound has almost faded when . . .

DORIS. Here! Line! . . .

Silence.

Fade in: Early morning sounds. In the foreground the rustle of newspaper.

WALTER. Alice . . . poor Alice . . .

Cut to: Interior. Sweet shop.

KEN JONES. This is everything she possessed, Mr Attard. My wife
picked them up this morning from a hostel in Archway where Alice
had been staying. She hated people knowing . . . about the hostel . . .
that's why we never gave you an address for her.

Pause.

I've looked through them. Only a few clothes. No documents or
letters . . . nothing like that.

WALTER. Thank you. I'm sorry. As I said I . . . I just came to return
the membership card . . . for the Bingo . . . and well . . . to say how

sorry I was.

KEN JONES. I appreciate that. There's going to be an inquest . . . the police don't seem to know whether it was a drunken driver . . . or hell raisers . . . or what. I don't know when the funeral is. There's no family you see . . .

WALTER. Yes . . . I'd like to be there. Thank you.

KEN JONES. Good day to you, then . . .

Fade out.

Fade in. Interior. Rolls Royce. Clay Street. Light traffic.

HILDA. There he is . . . coming out of the shop now. Pull over to the kerb will you?

The car draws smoothly to a halt. The window is automatically wound down with a gentle whirr. Street sounds infiltrate.

Mr Attard . . .

WALTER. Why . . . Miss Stewart!

HILDA. I must talk to you.

She opens the car door.

Please, I beg of you . . .

WALTER. At your office?

HILDA. No. My home at Barnes. I want to tell you the truth.

WALTER *gets into car. Car door is closed. Window whirrs up.*

Thank you, Mister Attard.

Car off.

Fade out.

Cut to: Interior. HILDA's *drawing room. She is dialling a telephone number.*

HILDA. If you knew what power you could have wielded over Crawfield Enterprises just by delving a little more and having a few less scruples. God, Arthur would have liked that little joke.

WALTER. I suppose so.

HILDA. Excuse me . . .

HILDA (*telephone*). Sarah. I'm at home. Get Oliver and Eric together in my office, will you. I want them to hear something. Call me back when they're ready.

She replaces the receiver . . . and lights a cigarette.

I want them to hear everything I shall say to you. They can stay in

my Clay Street office and listen over the telephone amplifier. That
way they can't interfere . . . and if they do . . . I can simply turn
their sound off.

Pause.

I loved Arthur deeply, you know. These are all his things. Ian is his
son. Did you know that?

WALTER. I guessed he was.

HILDA. I've never made a secret of it. Everything I've done for the
company has really been done for him. Not myself . . . no, not me
. . . and here I am about to throw it all away. C'est la vie and so on
and so forth.

Telephone rings.

Here we go.

Telephone is picked up. A click as HILDA *switches to amplification.
The voices of all those speaking over the amplified telephone are
loud, but have equally magnified distortion.*

SARAH (*distort*). Mr Hanwell and Mr Maybury are ready. I'm
putting you through.

Click.

HILDA. Thank you.

OLIVER (*distort*). Hilda . . .?

HILDA. Good morning, Oliver. Good morning, Eric.

ERIC (*distort*). What's all this about, Hilda?

HILDA. Mr Attard is with me.

OLIVER (*distort*). What's the matter?

HILDA. Nothing's the matter. I asked him here. I've decided to tell him
everything I know about the night Arthur was . . . 'disappeared'.

OLIVER (*distort*). You've decided to do . . . what?!

ERIC (*distort*). No . . . don't. Hilda . . . is Ian with you?

HILDA. There's only Mr Attard and myself.

ERIC (*distort*). You can't . . . you really can't . . .

OLIVER (*distort*). Listen Hilda . . . wait until we . . .

Click. HILDA *has turned off amplification.*

HILDA. I've turned you off, Oliver. The amplifier is off. I can't hear
you now and you'll never get here in time to stop me saying what I
am about to say. So please . . . just listen. Mr Attard knows most
of it anyway.

I think.

HILDA *shakes with nerves. During this scene she roams the room, as the words pour from her.*

Where to start . . .?

WALTER (*softly*). Is Arthur dead . . .?

HILDA. Yes . . . oh yes . . . he's dead. He is dead. He died on the sixteenth of August 1944. Had he lived Arthur Crawfield Ltd. would have pottered on like Walter Attard. Accountant. He was not a businessman. He could have taken you with him no place. When he died the firm and Arthur himself were in a dreadful state. He couldn't stand the strain and wanted out! But Oliver and Eric wanted the company to see the war through. They didn't want it dissolved . . . (*Shouting.*) . . . Did . . . you . . . Oliver!!! No, they wanted to hang on for the post-war boom. Then . . . manna from heaven . . . came. Arthur was offered a contract to build a small chemical factory for a German based drug company with the very English name of Athertons. No one else would touch them with a barge pole . . . and Arthur didn't want to know . . . but Oliver . . . has no scruples. And Eric . . . oh Eric as usual sat on the fence, waiting to be dragged over to the strongest side. He was. Oliver won. Then Arthur got clever. He pretended to fall in with their plans. He even fixed a date for the contract to be signed . . . August the seventeenth. But knowing full well, that on the previous evening . . . the sixteenth, he and I would be running away together. Leave them to stew. Get out with no scenes. No drama.

She laughs.

You see, the Company Charter stated that Arthur's signature must be on every contract, so without him, the company would be forced to disintegrate.

Pause.

But we didn't make it . . . the day that should have been the start of something good, was . . . was the last time I ever saw him . . .

WALTER. I'm sorry.

HILDA (*lighting a cigarette*). We all left the office at five-thirty that night. I came here alone . . . to Arthur's house. I don't know where Oliver and Eric said they were off to. Arthur went back to the office to pick up a few things . . . personal bits and pieces. He also said something about a document . . .

WALTER. Do you know what that document was?

HILDA. Well no . . . well, that night I waited here. This room is the same as it was then. My cases by the desk over there. He rang from the office at eight-fifteen to say he was about to leave. At nine he

hadn't arrived so I rang the office. The line was dead. I called the
operator. Clay Street had been razed to the ground. I sat in that
armchair all night. Right through dawn. At ten o'clock on
Thursday morning, I unpacked my suitcase.

Pause.

It was the seventeenth. The date the Atherton contract had to be
signed. No one knew where Arthur was. As far as Oliver and Eric
were concerned, Arthur had wanted the deal to go through. I was
so stunned I didn't know what to think. I was pregnant. What if
he wasn't in some hospital . . . what if he had died in the bombing
. . . I had no money . . . and with no offices even, the Atherton
contract was the only answer. . . Hitler money or not. Anyway . . .
we 'forged' Arthur's signature. I say 'we' because we all complied.
That was a grave error on my part. Once I'd gone along with that
contract, thus affirming that Arthur was alive on the seventeenth
. . . I could never in the future state that he had died on the
sixteenth without implicating myself in fraud. Also . . . without a
body and without a death certificate the company of Arthur
Crawfield Limited could never legally be dissolved. We had to keep
Arthur alive . . . while I had to smother any suspicions I had about
the way he died. But . . . whatever the cost, the contract was
signed. With the profits we formed new companies . . . until. . .
well . . . Crawfield International . . .

Silence. HILDA *sighs deeply. She speaks softly to* WALTER.

So . . .

She clicks on the amplifier.

OLIVER (*distort*). . . . Idea she was going to do anything like this, Eric?

HILDA. No one had any idea, Oliver.

OLIVER (*distort*). Well, congratulations.

HILDA. I think Eric is maybe relieved a little . . .

ERIC (*distort*). Are you, Hilda?

HILDA (*weakly*). Not enough . . . no . . . not nearly . . .

ERIC (*distort*). What do we do now?

HILDA *is softly crying.*

OLIVER (*distort*). Walter . . .?

WALTER. Yes?

HILDA (*harshly pulling herself together*). Oh please, for pity's sake,
Oliver . . . don't insult a gentleman by offering him money. That's
not Mr Attard's style.

ERIC (*distort*). Why today, Hilda? After all these years of covering up . . . why today?

HILDA. Because Alice Chapman was murdered last night.

OLIVER (*distort*). Killed in a car accident!

HILDA. An accident!? In a car park at the back of a Bingo Hall!

OLIVER (*distort*). Do you really think anyone would want to . . .

HILDA. She was murdered, Oliver.

OLIVER (*distort*). For what reason?

HILDA. I think she was murdered because she knew something about what happened the night Arthur disappeared that I, at least, do not know. Whoever killed her was afraid she would tell Mr Attard the truth of what happened that night.

ERIC (*distort*). You can't be right, Hilda . . .

OLIVER (*distort*). Do you know why anyone should want to kill Alice Chapman, Walter?

WALTER. I . . . I think I know of a possibility . . . yes . . .

ERIC (*distort*). Why . . . Mr Attard?

WALTER. Alice Chapman told me that her aunt was paid ten pounds a month from August, 1944 until the day she died, because of something she had seen or heard in Arthur's office on Wednesday the sixteenth. The ten pounds was always paid by postal order . . . from the same issuing office. Today . . . this afternoon, in fact, Alice was to give me the name of that issuing office, so that I could trace whoever paid that money out. As we know . . . she died before she could do so.

OLIVER (*distort*). So the ten pounds a month was blackmail . . . silence money?

WALTER. You must draw your own conclusions.

OLIVER (*distort*). Hilda obviously has.

HILDA. Yes.

OLIVER (*distort*). Blackmail for what. Silence about what?

HILDA. About who murdered Arthur.

OLIVER (*distort*). So somebody murdered Arthur? and what makes you think that?

HILDA (*quietly*). Don't patronise, Oliver . . . just don't. Arthur telephoned me from the office at eight-fifteen . . . exactly as arranged. He said he would leave the office immediately. The bombs didn't hit Clay Street until half an hour later, by which time he should have been well clear of the office and half way home . . .

here . . . to me . . . where he knew I was waiting. I believe somebody spoke to him *after* he had telephoned me . . . I believe they killed him . . . and that Alice discovered who that person was . . . what's more I believe that person is alive today and killed Alice.

WALTER. Miss Stewart . . . was Arthur's body found . . .?

HILDA. No body was found . . . many people died . . . and there were . . . there were traces of . . . but . . .

OLIVER (*distort*). And the motive for your lover's demise, Hilda . . . you still haven't told us why you think he may have been murdered . . . I suppose you've worked out something over the past thirty years through your cocaine haze.

HILDA. I've considered it.

OLIVER (*distort*). And I think I can guess at your conclusions.

HILDA. Can you?

OLIVER (*distort*). You think that we . . . Eric and me . . . or maybe just me. God knows you couldn't think it of Eric alone . . . knew that Arthur was planning to run out on us . . . and so on the night we knew he and you were eloping . . . we struck him down. Eh? Is that what you think? Is that why we're here in Clay Street and you're in Barnes, so that we can't commit triple murder? Don't worry, Walter . . .

He laughs.

You're quite safe . . . but here's another motive for murder. Perhaps Arthur decided he didn't want to be saddled with a neurotic mistress and child. Perhaps he told her . . . and maybe she dealt the death blow . . .

HILDA. I loved him. He meant more to me than anyone . . . or anything else in the world . . . then or now.

OLIVER (*distort*). Did he love you?

Pause. WALTER *speaks quietly.*

WALTER. Or maybe they were both what they appear . . . a man blown to bits by a bomb . . . and a woman killed in a car accident.

HILDA. No . . .

ERIC (*distort*). Well, what now, Mr Attard . . .?

WALTER. I shall return to my home . . . and think. Mr Maybury.

Pause.

I feel very sad . . . I feel tired . . . and old. The car that's been following me . . . I have noticed . . . the red mini . . . could I travel back in it, do you think? It's a long journey . . . and we'll both be going the same way.

HILDA. I . . . I'll speak to the driver.

WALTER. Thank you. Well, then . . . I shall say goodbye. Does anyone know what the document was that Arthur completed in his office that night?

HILDA. I said . . . I don't . . . Oliver . . . Eric?

ERIC (*distort*). No . . .

OLIVER (*distort*). I doubt there was one . . .

WALTER. Ah well then . . . good day, gentlemen . . .

Door opens. WALTER *and* HILDA *go into hallway and meet* IAN.

HILDA. Oh no . . .

IAN (*icily*). Mother . . .

WALTER. Why . . . Mr Stewart . . . Good Morning.

HILDA. I . . . Ian's just re-booked the car for another week, please use it . . . as you require it . . .

WALTER. Thank you.

Front door opens.

HILDA. Goodbye.

WALTER. Goodbye.

Front door closes.

HILDA. You heard, my darling?

IAN. Yes . . .

HILDA. Everything was for you . . . the forgery . . . I went along with it all for you . . . all of it . . . thirty odd years of . . .

IAN (*gently but still stunned*). It . . . it doesn't matter . . . but I'll find out who caused this . . .

HILDA. No . . . no Ian . . .

IAN. Oh but I will . . . (*he shouts.*) Oliver! Eric! Do you hear? I won't sit on my backside for another thirty-four years . . . counting the PENNIES! (*Softly.*) I'll make things right mother . . . you'll see . . .

Cut to: Interior. Red mini.

TERRY. Where to, old man?

WALTER. My name is Walter. Take me home.

TERRY (*starting car with difficulty*). Sorry . . . Walter. Home it is.

Car moves off noisily.

Cut to: Interior. WYN's *kitchen.*

WYN. I went over to pacify Miss Kirk this morning. You'll have to do something about her, Walter. Send her flowers or something . . .

WALTER. The document would tell us why . . . and the post office would tell us . . . who. Oh, Alice . . .

WYN. I picked up the post for you as well. Brought it back with me, I thought it would save her forwarding it . . . you're not listening are you?

WALTER. I'm sorry . . .?

WYN. It doesn't matter. Your post. Here . . . from the office.

WALTER. Oh . . .

WYN. All circulars, except for gas bill and picture postcard . . .

WALTER. Postcard . . . wonder who that's from . . .

He rifles through the post and finds card.

Piccadilly Circus Eh? (*Reading.*) 'Thanks for . . . winter coat . . . Post Office at . . . and Barclays Bank, Highbury . . .? (*Silence.*) Alice! By God . . . Barclays Bank, Highbury . . .

Cut to: Interior. Barclays Bank.

WALTER. Yes . . . it's thirty-four years ago. Arthur Crawfield is my name.

TELLER Do you know roughly what date the document was deposited with us?

WALTER. Yes . . . the evening of the sixteenth of August 1944 I think.

TELLER. If you could take a seat for a moment, Mr Crawfield. It may take us a while.

WALTER. Thank you . . .

Fade out.

Fade in.

TELLER. Mr Crawfield. I've looked, sir, but we have nothing at all deposited by you on the sixteenth . . .

WALTER. Ah . . . I thought . . . I must be mistaken. I'm sorry to have . . .

TELLER. We do have a document for you that you brought in on the seventeenth of August.

WALTER. The seventeenth? That *I* brought in?

TELLER. Yes . . . here we are.

WALTER. But that's impossible. *I* brought it in on the seventeenth?

TELLER. Why, yes, sir. Do you want to take it away now?

WALTER. . . . er . . . yes . . . yes please.

TELLER. It's a bit grubby I'm afraid. If you would just sign for it, Mr Crawfield.

WALTER. Oh . . . of course . . . yes. I . . . er . . . don't expect my penmanship will have improved with age.

He writes.

Bit shakier.

TELLER. There we are, then. Thank you, Mr Crawfield.

Fade out.

Fade in. Street sounds . . . but a little distant. Children at play. WALTER in foreground.

WALTER. Now Arthur, my old friend . . . what clues did you leave me, eh? Lets see . . .

Envolope is opened. Pause. The rustle of paper.

(*Reading.*) To whom it may . . . (*Pause.*)

He laughs gently to himself.

Well, I never . . . oh Arthur . . .

Fade out on his gentle laughter.

Mini car door opens. Interior. Car.

TERRY. There you are, old man. I thought I'd lost you.

WALTER. Yes, I'm sorry about that. I got delayed. Shopping.

TERRY. That's all right. Had a phone call to make myself.

Door closes. Carrier bag put down.

WALTER. Three champagne glasses, a bottle of the very best champagne and a map of England.

TERRY. Where are we going now?

WALTER. Later we have quite a long journey. But first . . . we're going to a party.

Cut to: Interior. WYN's kitchen. WALTER is excited and happy.

WALTER. We can't stay for more than a few minutes.

WYN. What's happening? Who've you got out there?

WALTER. He's a friend of mine. He has rather an unfortunate habit of calling me 'old man' but apart from that . . . you'll like him.

WYN. Where are you rushing off to?

WALTER. Never mind about that.

WYN. But . . .

WALTER. Ssssh . . .

WYN. What have you brought him here with you for?

WALTER. I had to see you first. I promised you something and I thought . . . oh God . . . if I don't do it tonight, she'll think I'm procrastinating again . . . and the next day . . . and the next day . . .

WYN. What? (*Pause.*) Come on. What is it? What are you up to?

WALTER. Well, it's like this . . .

He laughs. Then WYN *laughs with him.*

WYN. What are you laughing at? Oh come on, Walter. What are you up to?

WALTER. You know.

WYN (*gently*). I don't know . . .

WALTER *takes out a ring box.*

WALTER. Dear Wyn . . . please . . . will you be my wife?

WYN (*barely audible*). Oh . . .

WALTER. Come on. What do you say . . .? (*Pause.*) Eh . . .?

WYN. Yes . . . please . . .

Door opens. Pop of a champagne cork.

TERRY. Here we are, Walter, old man . . . bubbly time . . .

General laughter. Then fade out.

Fade up street outside the house. It is some time later. The faint sound of WYN *and* WALTER's *laughter emanates from their house. Inside his car, in the foreground,* IAN STEWART *groans with boredom and impatience as he lights a cigarette.*

IAN (*Whistles*).

Front door of house opens and closes TERRY's *footsteps approach from the front door and* IAN *calls him urgently, softly.*

Fisher . . .!

TERRY. Stone me. It's you . . . you half scared me to death. I couldn't get away earlier. Besides there was nothing to tell you.

IAN. But there is now . . .?

TERRY (*after a pause, almost reluctantly*). Yes . . . I've told them I'm getting the map from the car.

IAN. Does he know I followed you from the bank?

TERRY. No.

IAN. This post office . . . where is it, then?

TERRY. Oake Earsby . . .

IAN. What?

TERRY. It's a place called Oake Earsby.

IAN. Where's that?

TERRY. You'd better look it up on a map. It's in Yorkshire.

IAN. Fine. I'll set off now . . . don't rush up there will you?

Car starts up.

Attard's looking for the man who killed a friend he hasn't seen for forty years . . . I'm looking for whoever killed my father.

TERRY. Well, good luck then, mate.

Car moves off. TERRY *sighs.*

Fade out.

Fade in. WYN's *kitchen and hallway.*

WALTER. We must go now. Heavens . . . we've been almost two hours . . .

WYN. Is it that long? I suppose it is.

WALTER. I must finish this business, eh Terry?

TERRY. Right on!

WYN. Of course . . . your adventure . . .

WALTER. Don't look so worried . . .

WYN. I'm not worried . . . oh really, Walter . . . put your coat on . . . and you, Terry (*Pause.*) There. Now have you got that map . . .?

TERRY. Yes, Mrs Fletcher.

Door opens. WYN *speaks tenderly.*

WYN. Oh my dear Walter, whatever you're going to do . . . take care . . .

They embrace and kiss.

WALTER. The end of my adventure Wyn, eh? The end of the adventure!

Cut to: Interior. Mini car. It starts with difficulty.

TERRY. Oake Earsby. It's a long drive, you know. The other side of Bradford.

WALTER. Yes . . .

Pause.

The best years of my life have been spent in that house with Wyn . . . the best and the happiest.

Pause.

Mrs Walter Attard . . .

Fade out.

Fade in. Very early morning village sounds . . . Birdsong in the foreground. The rustle of mars bar paper.

WALTER. I've got the address from them. We're off.

TERRY. Where is it?

WALTER. Not far.

TERRY. Did you get me another Mars bar?

Car door opens. They get inside.

WALTER. I did . . . somewhere . . . here . . .

TERRY. What's the hurry? They won't be up yet.

Car starts again with difficulty.

WALTER. Yes . . . I fear they will. Someone's been here before us.

Car moves off. Fade out.

Fade in as car door slams.

TERRY. All roses round my door, eh?

WALTER. Wait here, Terry.

TERRY. As you say, old man.

WALTER moves slowly up a garden path. He reaches a door and knocks, there is no response.

Cut to: Interior. Cottage. A clock ticks loudly and a cat purrs. In the foreground a gun is cocked and loaded. It is then placed in a drawer which slides partially shut.

There is another knock on the door, and then it slowly opens. The cat mews and runs. We hear the voice of ARTHUR CRAWFIELD, sad but friendly and gentle.

ARTHUR. Come in, Walter . . . and close the door.

The door is closed. WALTER approaches a little.

I saw you coming up the garden path. I recognised you instantly.

WALTER (*his quest over*). Arthur Crawfield . . .

ARTHUR. It's George Rochester now, Walter. Has been for many years. How did you find me . . .?

WALTER. I promised myself I'd find you.

ARTHUR. I thought there was no way any more.

WALTER. Alice.

ARTHUR. Alice Chapman?

WALTER. Whoever killed her was too late. She had a change of heart.

ARTHUR. Ah . . .

WALTER. A picture postcard. (*Pause.*) Post Office. Oake Earsby.

ARTHUR. Then may she go to heaven.

ARTHUR *laughs gently.* WALTER *goes to step forward.*

No . . . stay there, Walter. I can see you well there . . .

WALTER. Have you lived here since '44?

ARTHUR. Yes . . . I worked in Bradford for a time. Oh . . . an accountant. You know . . . small firm . . . little fish . . . little pool . . . that's my style . . .

WALTER. An accountant, eh?

ARTHUR. I retired a few months ago.

WALTER. I retired a few days ago.

ARTHUR. Well . . . there's a thing . . .

WALTER. I wanted to talk to you . . .

ARTHUR. So . . . here we are . . . (*Pause.*) Not far from Haworth here . . .

WALTER. No . . .

ARTHUR. The Brontes. See . . . I remembered.

WALTER. Yes . . .

ARTHUR. Won't you sit down, my old friend, please . . .

WALTER (*sitting down*). You came up here on the seventeenth?

ARTHUR. Yes. I'd hired a car.

WALTER. The blue car was yours?

ARTHUR. Blue? was it blue? Yes . . . my, how did you know that? I hired it for three days. Complete with driver. A last luxury . . . a last business perk from Arthur Crawfield Ltd.

WALTER. Did you ever mean to take Hilda with you?

ARTHUR. I thought of it . . . but not for Hilda's sake . . . but the child she was carrying. I couldn't cope with Hilda any more than I could cope with the business.

Pause.

Oh, I don't know . . . it was all up here . . . in my head . . . beyond me. The idea of everything was always so much easier than putting it into practice.

WALTER. Yes, I know.

Pause.

ARTHUR. Did you ever get married, Walter?

WALTER. I'm engaged.

ARTHUR. Oh . . . almost then.

Pause.

Edith Emson helped me that night on the 16th. She was a good woman. Did you know she'd helped me? I'd had some threatening letters about the Atherton contract. Everyone seemed to know they were backed with German money. Already somebody had thrown bricks through the barber's shop window below. Well, as luck would have it, just as I was about to leave the office, they came for me . . . that's how this happened . . . see . . . the scar? They threw milk bottles through the office window, they knocked me out, Walter. There was blood everywhere . . . not just a scratch. Then suddenly Edith arrived. She'd returned from the shelter to pick up her handbag or something . . . anyway, she helped me to the car. I was in such a bad shape, I didn't know what precisely I would do. So . . . I told Edith that if Miss Stewart was to ask my whereabouts the next day, then Edith was to tell her to contact Barclays Bank, Highbury, where she would find a document.

WALTER. . . . in which you gave her power of attorney to take over all your interests in Arthur Crawfield Limited. She could sign for you . . .

ARTHUR. Yes . . . I intended leaving her, but I would give her everything I had. But you see when Edith spoke to Hilda. Hilda lied. She said she'd seen me and spoken to me. So did Eric. So did Oliver . . . (*He laughs.*) . . . so Edith never passed on the message. They thought I was dead . . . and they forged my name.

WALTER. You did nothing . . .

ARTHUR. I wanted to do nothing. I was not going to give up my new anonymity . . . for them. Let them live with their frauds. They'd betrayed all I started out to achieve. The only thing is I paid Edith Emson ten pounds a month as a payment for her to say nothing . . . and also for news of my son.

Pause.

That continued until the day she died. I heard of her death from Alice.

Pause.

Have you met my son, Walter?

WALTER. Yes.

ARTHUR. I've heard nothing about him since Edith died. I've never seen a photograph.

Pause.

Everything had passed smoothly. Then, with your help, Alice put two and two together. She knew much more than she'd told you. She rang me. She said she'd been offered seventy-five pounds . . .

WALTER. Forty . . . it was forty . . .

ARTHUR. And I would have to pay her much more than that to keep her quiet. (*Pause.*) Well, I couldn't let her reveal the fraud . . . not for Ian . . . so I decided to kill her. It was easy in a car. No contact . . . just a . . . a three point turn . . .

WALTER. Yes . . .

WALTER *starts to rise.*

. . . there's a car at the back . . .

ARTHUS. Don't move . . . stay there, Walter . . .!

WALTER. But I . . .

ARTHUR. Please listen . . .

Pause.

Someone came here this morning . . . before you . . . that is their car. They . . . they came to kill me . . . because they thought I had murdered Arthur Crawfield . . . I couldn't say anything . . . they accused me of . . . murdering myself . . .

WALTER. Did they go to the police? Who was it?

ARTHUR. I want you to tell me.

WALTER. What?

ARTHUR *takes out the gun.*

ARTHUR. He brought this to kill me. We struggled . . . and he died. The gun went off.

WALTER. Where is he??

ARTHUR. He's here . . . at my feet .... behind this desk.

He moves away.

You can look there and tell me.

WALTER *crosses to the desk.*

WALTER. Oh God . . .

ARTHUR (*barely audible*). Is that Ian? Have I killed my son?

Pause.

WALTER. It is your son . . . yes.

Pause.

ARTHUR. On the table in the kitchen there's an envelope Walter. Would you fetch it?

WALTER. Yes . . .

WALTER *goes into the kitchen.*

ARTHUR. It's a confession by myself to the murders of Alice Chapman and Ian.

Pause.

There's nothing you can say . . . is there? What can you say to a man who's killed his son. There was no peace, really, Walter, you know. There was never peace.

The gun is cocked.

Goodbye, my friend . . .

The gun is fired. The reverberation mixes with the sound of TERRY *calling.*

TERRY. Walter!! Walter !!

The reverberations continue. Voices fade. Birdsong takes over. Sounds of the rose garden as opening of play. Footsteps on gravel. Those of WYN *and* WALTER.

WALTER. I walked through these gardens every day of my working life, Wyn . . . I know every flower . . . every tree . . . every shrub . . . longing for adventure.

WYN. That adventure's over now, Walter . . .

WALTER. What time is it . . .?

WYN. Fifteen minutes to eleven . . .

WALTER. Fifteen minutes to go . . .

WYN. Five minutes walk . . .

WALTER. That's all.

GARDENER. 'Morning Mr Attard . . .

WALTER. Good morning.

WYN (*softly*). Mustn't be late.

GARDENER. What's that in your button-hole?

WALTER. Mary Rose.

GARDENER. Quite correct, Mr Attard.

WALTER. Ten out of ten . . .

WYN. You haven't forgotten the ring, have you, Walter . . .?

WALTER. No, Wyn, I haven't forgotten the ring . . .

Theme music.

The end.

AFTERNOON THEATRE
THE CHILD

by Olwen Wymark

For Pat

The Child was first broadcast on BBC Radio 4 on 24th October 1979.
The cast was as follows:

GEMMA	Miriam Margolyes
NINA	Jane Wenham
LILY	Mary Wimbush
POLICEMAN	Danny Schiller
POLICE WOMAN	Lolly Cockerell

Director: Richard Wortley

Olwen Wymark is an American living in London. She has written a
number of radio and stage plays, many of which have been produced in
London and the provinces, and several in America. In 1956 her play
The Unexpected Country won a BBC *Writing for Sound* competition.
The Ransom and *California Here I Come* were among her other plays
broadcast by the BBC. Her first stage play, *Lunchtime Concert*, was
produced at the Glasgow Citizen's Theatre in 1966.

This was followed by *Loved* which was staged at the Bush Theatre in
1978 and in America in 1979, and *Find Me*, which was adapted for radio
and broadcast in America where it won an award, and subsequently by
the BBC. Of the many one-act plays Olwen Wymark has written, eight
have been published by John Calder in two volumes, *The Gymnasium
and Other Plays* and *Three Plays*. Her writing for television includes
Love Story and *Crown Court*.

NINA (*calling*). Gemma. Gemma.

Then we are inside, hearing her call in the distance.

Gemma. Gemma.

GEMMA. She thinks I'm still outside playing in the garden. (*Sharply.*) Don't look away!

LILY. I didn't. Why don't you answer her?

GEMMA. Oh she'll find me. Now. It's my turn. What I see in your eyes, Lily, is two tiny tiny little babies all curled up. One in each eye in the black middle part. They're sleeping. No, they're dead I think. (*Quickly.*) Did you smile?

LILY (*calm*). No.

NINA (*outside. Calling*). Gemma. Gemma.

LILY. Answer her, Gemma.

GEMMA. No I don't want to. She'll come in here and ask you where I am anyway. What do you see in my eyes, Lily? It's your turn.

LILY. Well . . . I can see a jungle.

GEMMA. That's because my eyes are green. What else?

LILY. Little orange monkeys swinging in the trees and making horrible faces at each other . . . you smiled.

GEMMA. I didn't! I didn't!

LILY. All right you didn't.

A door opens.

NINA. Lily, do you know where . . . oh there you are, Gemma. I've been calling and calling.

GEMMA. We heard you. 'Gemma! Gemma!'

LILY. I told her to answer you.

NINA. What on earth are you two doing? Sitting there staring at each other. (*She laughs.*)

GEMMA (*fierce*). Don't mummy. Stop. You might make us laugh. That's the game. You have to go on looking straight into the other one's eyes and the first one that smiles or laughs loses. Or if you look away you lose. Can you still see those monkeys, Lily?

LILY. Yes, and I think I can see Tarzan.

GEMMA. I made you see Tarzan. I was thinking about him and you saw him in my thoughts. (*Dreamy.*) And all the monkeys are inside my head. My go again. Your eyes have turned into two guns pointing at me.

LILY. Oh? What happened to the babies?

GEMMA. They fell backwards out of your eyes and now they're inside your ears. They fell all the way down into your ear holes. Can you hear them crying?

LILY. I thought you said they were dead.

GEMMA. They were only pretending. They wanted you to go to the Doctor and say 'Good God, Doctor, what shall I do? I've got two tiny dead babies in my eyes.' You laughed.

LILY (*laughing*). Good God Doctor . . .

NINA. Well I don't think it's funny. What a creepy game.

GEMMA. I won! I won! Let's play again.

NINA. Not now. It's supper time. I was calling you for supper.

LILY. Righto Nina. Come along, Gemma.

GEMMA. I don't want supper. I want to play.

NINA. You can go on playing afterwards.

GEMMA. No! Now! Now! Now!

NINA. Now Gemma, don't be silly.

GEMMA (*intense rage*). Shut up you! I don't do what you say. I do what I say. Now! Now! I want to play now!

NINA. Be a good girl, Gemma. It's sausages for supper.

GEMMA. I hate sausages and I hate you. If you don't let me play I'll smash up all the furniture in here. I will! I'll break the windows. I'll burn this house down. (*Malevolent.*) I'll kill you. I'll kill both of you.

LILY (*dramatic*). Oh quick Nina, get down on your knees with me. Gemma says she's going to kill us. We must plead with her. Please, Gemma, please don't kill us. (*Aside. Low.*) Nina . . .

NINA. Oh all right. (*Dramatic.*) Please please don't kill Lily and me, Gemma.

GEMMA (*shouts wildly*). I will. I'm going to. You can't stop me!

LILY (*dramatic*). Oh Nina has she got a gun? I'm afraid to look. I'm so afraid!

NINA (*dramatic*). Yes she has! She's got a gun in her hand. What are we going to do? She'll shoot us!

GEMMA (*laughing, excited, triumphant*). Yes! Here's my gun! Look out I'm going to shoot your eyes out.

LILY (*pretending to cry*). No no no!

GEMMA. Yes! And I'm going to shoot your noses off and your stomachs and your legs and your teeth. I'm going to shoot you into pieces.

NINA. Oh stop her, Lily. I'm afraid.

LILY. We can't stop her. Nobody can stop Gemma. She's too strong for us, Nina.

GEMMA. Yes, yes I am. I'm the strongest in the whole world. Here I go. Look out. Bang! Bang! Bang! Bang! Bang bang!

LILY *and* NINA *make exaggerated dying sounds and we hear them fall on the floor. Silence.*

GEMMA (*in a little sing song voice*). Dead dead dead. Mummy's dead and Lily's dead. Dead dead dead.

We hear her move across the room.

GEMMA (*giggling*). Now I can tickle them because they're dead. (*Excitedly.*) Tickle tickle tickle tickle!

LILY *and* NINA *are laughing helplessly.*

NINA. Stop stop! Oh I can't bear it. Stop, Gemma.

LILY. Quick Nina. Help me grab her. We'll tickle her.

There is a scuffle.

LILY. I've got her!

NINA. Tickle tickle tickle.

GEMMA (*laughing*). Mummy, mummy, stop tickling! Stop!

LILY. Are we alive again? Eh? Are we alive Gemma?

NINA. Tickle tickle tickle.

GEMMA (*shouting and laughing*). Yes yes! You're alive again.

LILY. Good. Then we'll stop.

They all subside, giggling and panting.

GEMMA (*sighs contentedly*). We're all alive and we can all go and have our supper.

NINA (*languid*). Those sausages'll be burned to a crisp. Shall we go down to the beach tomorrow morning?

GEMMA. Yes! Yes yes!

LILY. We can't We've already been this week. Once a week is the rule.

GEMMA. We can. We can. I want to get some more treasure.

NINA. It is a week, Lily. It was last Friday we went and tomorrow's Thursday.

LILY (*grunting as she gets up*). Oh Gawd. Up at four-thirty a.m. then is it? I'm too old for all this larking about.

NINA (*gets up*). Fuss fuss. It's only once a week. You sleep till noon every other day. It's all that whiskey you drink in the evenings. Up you get, Gemma.

LILY (*mild*). If I didn't drink the whiskey I wouldn't sleep at all what with this one running up and down the stairs and banging all the doors.

GEMMA. Nobody plays with me in the night.

NINA. How can you say that, Gemma? I read to you for hours last night.

GEMMA. Yes but you kept falling asleep. Right in the middle of the story . . . (*Makes loud snoring noise.*)

LILY. Well, you let your mother and me sleep tonight if you want to go to the beach tomorrow morning. Will you?

GEMMA. I'll try.

LILY. Good girl.

NINA. She is. She's a good girl.

LILY (*laughs*). She's always a good girl after she kills us, aren't you Gemma?

GEMMA (*dreamy*). Yes. I shot you all to pieces.

NINA. Come along. Supper.

GEMMA. And tomorrow the beach!

Sound of waves breaking quite loud.

GEMMA (*breathless chanting under the sound of the sea*). Can't catch me for a bumble bee. Can't catch me for a bumble bee. Come and get me, waves! See how close I am? I'm getting closer and closer. If you want to you can knock me down. You can drown me. You can eat me up. Come on, come on, I dare you. (*Then running and laughing.*) You missed me! I've got away from you. Stupid old sea, you can't catch me.

Then the sound of the waves from a distance.

NINA. Look at her down there. She never gets tired of that game.

LILY. Mmmm . . . What?

NINA. Were you asleep, Lily? I don't know how you can. It's so cold.

LILY. I'm not asleep. I just go into a coma. I'm trying to imagine I'm back in bed. I wish to God we could come down here when the sun's up.

NINA. Oh Lily, you know we can't. Not when there are people. We can't.

LILY. I know, I know.

NINA. Besides, the sun is up.

LILY. Only just.

NINA. Well it's very beautiful, Lily, you must admit.

LILY *yawns.*

NINA (*romantically*). Dawn over the sea. Look at the sky. Such wonderful colours. I wish I was a painter.

LILY. I wish I was back in bed.

NINA. Oh Lily, do you hate it so much.

LILY. No of course I don't. Stop looking so guilty, Nina. I'm just having a little grumble. Keeps me warm.

NINA. Well I feel guilty sometimes. She's not your child. You put up with so much, Lily. It worries me.

LILY (*affectionate*). Shut your face. Put up? Where would I be without you two, eh? Back in London in that horrible little bedsitter in the Euston Road. Lonely. Miserable as sin. Besides, she feels like my child. Ours. Our child.

NINA (*grateful*). Yes.

LILY Look at her. She's doing one of her dances.

NINA. She'll get terribly wet.

LILY. She always does. Never mind. We've got the blanket to wrap her up in. Did you remember a plastic bag for the treasure?

NINA. Yes I've got it. Goodness knows where we'll put any more. The house is bursting with rocks and bits of glass and sticks. And she'll never let me throw a thing out. She seems to know every piece of it.

LILY. Well it is treasure to her. Look at her go, Nina. The whirling dervish. Funny, isn't it, anyone else looking at her now . . . ridiculous they'd think. Prancing around like that . . . singing her head off too, she will be. But somehow or other she looks beautiful to me.

NINA. Yes. It's because she's happy.

Sound of waves loud again and GEMMA's *voice under it singing a tuneless wordless song. Cut sound. Silence. Then* GEMMA *whimpering and moaning.*

GEMMA. Where is she where is she? I can't see her anywhere. She's gone. She's gone.

LILY. Stop it, Gemma. Come away from the window. She'll come back. She's only gone shopping. Doesn't she always come back?

GEMMA (*wails*). I don't know!

LILY. Try and remember. Sometimes I go out shopping and sometimes Mummy goes. We go away for a little while and then we come back. With all kinds of lovely food.

GEMMA. And sweeties?

LILY. And sweeties. You see, you do remember. Now come away from the window. We'll go and put on a kettle so Mummy can have a nice cup of tea when she comes back.

Sound of a kettle being filled from the tap.

LILY. Oh now. Look at you. Silly girl. Why do you want to be under the table?

GEMMA. It's better here. You come under too, Lily.

LILY. Oh Gemma, I don't want to. I'm too fat to fit under there.

GEMMA. No you're not, you're not. Please Lily. Look, I'm all small in the corner. There's hundreds and hundreds of room for you. Please Lily come and be with me. We'll be all right under here. (*Whispers.*) Then if they come they won't see us.

LILY. They? Who's they?

GEMMA. Shhh! Don't. (*Low. Urgent.*) Don't talk about them. You mustn't. If they hear you they could come. Crashing through the walls. They would, Lily.

LILY. Well I'd stop them. I'd say . . . who do you think you are crashing through our walls. Just you go back where you came from I'd say. Leave our walls alone do you hear? I'd scare them off, don't you worry about that.

GEMMA (*moaning*). No you can't, you can't stop them. They're too big. Lily please come under here with me. I'm afraid.

LILY. All right, all right. I'll just turn the kettle down low. There. Now when the whistle goes . . . (*Grunts as she starts getting under the table.*) I'm never going to fit under here. Move your foot, Gemma. Ough. Now I've bumped my head. As soon as that kettle whistle goes we come out, right, Promise?

GEMMA. Yes I do. I do promise. See . . . isn't it nice under here? Now we're both together and we're safe. They can't hear us now if we whisper. (*Whispers.*) Listen Lily, listen. They've got faces like lions do only they're not yellow — they're black and all scaley. And they're bigger than this house and they've got wings, great big wings. Do you know what the wind is, Lily? That's their wings flapping back and forth. You and Mummy say 'don't be frightened it's only the wind' but it isn't. It's their wings flapping back and forth and up and down.

LILY. My gracious is that really true?

GEMMA. Yes. I've watched them out of the window at night when you and Mummy are asleep. You can see their teeth shining in the moonlight when they smile.

LILY. Ugh.

GEMMA. Are you frightened of them, Lily?

LILY. Yes I am. Horrible things.

GEMMA. Are you shivering and shaking?

LILY. My goodness yes. Brrrrrr!

GEMMA (*laughs*). I made them up. I just made them up out of my head.

LILY. You never did.

GEMMA (*laughing*). Yes.

LILY. It was just a trick to get me under the table, wasn't it?

GEMMA. Yes. You believed me. You were scared, weren't you Lily?

LILY. You're an awful girl. Always frightening the life out of us with your stories. You're naughty.

GEMMA (*serious*). No I'm not, Lily. It isn't naughty. If you make it into a story and you can scare somebody else with it then it goes away.

LILY. Oh is that what happens.

GEMMA. Yes. Now you tell me a story.

LILY. All right. Just a minute . . . let me think. Um . . . once upon a time there was a silly fat woman who had a rope around her neck. It was tied in a loop with a big strong knot and the end of the rope trailed on the ground. Everywhere she went the rope dragged along behind her. She lived all alone in a dark smelly little room and she didn't know anybody. When she went out to buy a bottle of milk or a bit of cheese all the cars and the buses and the lorries went banging and rushing by but nobody looked at her. Nobody talked to her. At night time she could never sleep. She lay awake listening to the cats fighting and yowling in the graveyard next door. And she was always thinking 'if only I could find a big tree and climb up it then I could tie the end of this rope to a strong branch and then I could jump off the branch.'

The kettle whistles.

Out we get.

Cut whistle. Sounds of water and clothes being washed.

NINA. Anymore sheets to be mangled, Lily.

LILY. No that's the lot. Phew I'm tired. What about a cup of coffee? We can leave the towels to soak for a bit.

NINA. I'll just hang these sheets out first. Lovely wind for drying this morning. You put the kettle on, Lily.

LILY. Where's Gemma?

NINA. In the garden in her Wendy House. I'll take her out a biscuit. Hasn't she been quiet today.

LILY. Mmmmm. Not a peep out of her since breakfast. How was she last night? I didn't hear her.

NINA. She sat up all night on the window seat in my room I don't know if she slept. She was just sitting there like a statue when I dropped off.

LILY. Amazes me the way she can go without sleep.

NINA. She's always been like that, even as a baby. Hand me the clothespegs will you?

LILY. Shall I give you a hand with the hanging out?

NINA. No no, I can manage.

LILY. Got Gemma's biscuit?

NINA. In my pinny pocket.

The back door opens and closes. LILY *is singing rather tunelessly to herself as she fills the kettle and gets out cups.*

NINA (*from outside, shouting*). Lily! Lily come quickly!

LILY (*going out doors*). Whatever is it Nina? What's wrong Nina, where are you?

NINA (*calling, frantic*). In here with Gemma. In the Wendy House. She's hurt herself!

Cut and in.

GEMMA (*flat monotonous*). No no no no no no no.

She continues doing this throughout the scene.

NINA. I'll never forgive myself for forgetting to put away those scissors. Oh Lily, the blood, look at all the blood.

LILY. It's all right, Nina. They're only scratches. (*Crooningly.*) Well Gemma, silly girl. There there now. There there. Let Lily wash your leg. Lovey.

NINA. Yes. Sit on Mummy's lap, Darling, while Lily washes your poor leg. That's the way. Oh what a heavy girl.

LILY. Just hold that towel there, Nina, while I get the bandages.

NINA. Yes I've got it. Gemma? Gemma. She doesn't even see us, Lily. What's she staring at? Gemma? What is it, darling? Tell Mummy.

GEMMA (*as before*). No no no no no no no.

LILY. It's the shock. Poor little girl, eh? Now we'll put some nice cool cream on these cuts. That's it. And then round and round with the bandage. And a bit of sticky plaster. There we go. All done. I'll get her a cup of hot sweet tea. Here, put my cardy round her, Nina, she's shivering. That's right.

Her footsteps going out.

GEMMA (*continuing*). No no no no no no.

NINA. Oh lambey, why did you do it? Why?

GEMMA *stops saying no. There is a pause.*

GEMMA (*flat. Expressionless*). They told me to. They made me. I told them no but they made me.

Door opens.

LILY. Oh, there you are . . .

NINA. She's asleep.

LILY. Good. Sit down, Nina, you look exhausted.

NINA. I am. (*Sighs as she sits.*) Oh what a day. I thought she'd never go off. What time is it?

LILY. Nearly midnight. You've been up there hours. You should have let me take another turn with her.

NINA. No no. You had her the whole afternoon. Playing with her. You were marvellous. I'm sorry I went to pieces like that.

LILY. Well it was a dreadful shock finding her like that. No wonder.

NINA. It was the feeling that . . . well you know. She's been so happy and contented lately. She has, hasn't she?

LILY. Yes, she has.

NINA. I just thought . . . when I saw her lying there just staring . . . all the blood. I thought, no matter how hard we try, how much we . . . I mean we're helpless in the end, we are!

LILY. Now now, Nina. We do what we can.

NINA. Yes. (*Tired.*) Poor child . . . oh poor child. How long ago was it . . . the other time?

LILY. Oh I don't know . . . five years? I can't remember. But that was much worse, much much worse. How she didn't blind herself!

NINA. We thought she had at first, remember? Oh God, the blood pouring down her face. I never thought she'd do anything like that again. Lily. I was so sure she wouldn't Oh why did she? If only we knew why.

LILY. Now Nina, how many times have we said it? There are things about Gemma we'll never understand. We can't.

NINA. I know. Yes I know.

LILY. Now. What about a nip of my whiskey? Your cocoa's in the thermos but I do think a little drink would do you good.

NINA. Oh no I don't think . . . Yes I will.

LILY. That's the way. (*Pours drinks.*)

NINA. Just a small one, Lily, really.

LILY. There you are. One thing we do know, Nina. We do know she's happier with us than she ever was in that hospital.

NINA. Oh I know that's true. Of course I do. It's only sometimes I . . . Well cheers or bottoms up or whatever you say.

LILY (*cheerful*). Down the hatch.

NINA. Oh, I can feel that going right down to the pain in my back. It's sitting all bent over like that for so long. You have to keep so still. Hardly dare to breathe while you're patting her or she's wide awake again. Even if you change the rhythm. I patted her four thousand four hundred and forty four times.

LILY. My God.

NINA. Well four's my lucky number. Four thousand four hundred and forty-four. Four fours in a row, you see.

LILY (*laughs a bit sadly*). Oh Nina Nina. Sometimes I think we're getting as mad as Gemma.

NINA (*firmly*). She's not mad, Lily. Disrupted. That's what they said that first time at the clinic.

LILY (*mild*). Long time ago. How old was she then? Four?

NINA. Yes, but she hasn't changed.

LILY. No. (*Pause.*) No she hasn't.

NINA. I blame that hospital, Lily, I always will.

LILY. Yes.

NINA. It made her worse. I knew it would. I told him and told him but he wouldn't listen.

LILY. I know.

NINA. She was like a little zombie in there. Never talked. Wouldn't play.

LILY. It's all those drugs.

NINA. He never went to see her. Not once. I'd make that journey every week . . . I'd say to him 'come with me. Why don't you some with me?' but he wouldn't. I'd beg him.

LILY. Poor little Gemma.

NINA. He was ashamed of her, you see. That was the thing that hurt me worst. I couldn't stop him putting her in there, you know. I tried. Legally. I couldn't.

LILY. Don't think about it. It's over now.

NINA. Do you know it was the first thing I thought. When de died. 'Now I can go and get her home again.' I wasn't thinking about him at all. Wicked, I suppose.

LILY. Not wicked, why? It was wicked of him to take her away from you. I'm glad I never met him.

NINA. When you think, Lily. Life's so strange. All those years and years never seeing each other, you and I, and now here we are.

LILY. Staying up half the night talking the way we did at school.

NINA (*laughs*). Only no whiskey then.

LILY. No. Not that we couldn't have used it. Remember how cold it always was?

NINA. Do I! And that awful Matron prowling about all the time. Do you remember how she used to spit when she talked?

LILY. And those terrible thick glasses that you couldn't see her eyes through. Beastly vicious woman she was. She used to really enjoy the canings. Some kind of sexual thrill for her I'll be bound.

NINA (*laughs*). Oh Lily!

LILY. No I mean it. You could hear her sort of panting while she was doing it. Honestly. You never got caned did you?

NINA. Once.

LILY. What for?

NINA. Wetting the bed. It was the first week I was there.

LILY. Oh God what an awful school that was.

NINA. Why didn't we write to each other after we left?

LILY. We did for a bit, don't you remember?

NINA. Well why did we stop?

LILY. Oh I don't know. The war . . .

NINA. I suppose.

LILY. Have another little drop.

NINA. I'm sure I shouldn't. I've never had any head for drink. I feel woozy already.

LILY. Well that won't hurt. Help you sleep. (*Gets up. Pours drinks.*) Nothing the matter with drink. Keeps the devil away.

NINA. You always say that. You don't really believe in the devil.

LILY. Oh I do. Cheers.

NINA. Cheers. No, I mean really believe.

LILY. So do I. I've never been too sure about God but I don't have any doubts about the devil. Every night when the sun goes down there he is waiting for me.

NINA. Waiting for you? What do you mean?

LILY. Nothing. Nothing at all. It's the whiskey talking. Take no notice.

NINA. Well you ought to believe in God, Lily. Don't you think it was Him that put you on the train that day?

LILY. What? That was Satan himself. There I was lying in bed that morning waiting for the sum to come up and wondering how I was going to get through another day when he whispered right in my ear. 'Just you go and catch a train to the seaside and when you get there you can fill the pockets of your old coat with stones and walk out into the sea and that'll be that.' You wouldn't catch God saying a thing like that, surely.

NINA (*laughs*). No but don't you see? God knew I'd be walking past the station just when you got off that train. He had it all planned out. (*Serious.*) I mean really Lily, it was wasn't it? Like a miracle.

LILY. It was a miracle you recognised me. I'll never understand that. I couldn't think who you were.

NINA (*laughs*). Pulling at your coat. Crying. We must have been a sight. You standing so still staring at me. You were like somebody in a trance.

LILY. Well I couldn't take it in. It'd been years and years since anybody had ever called me my name.

NINA. Oh Lily. I can't bear to think of how lonely you were all that time.

LILY. Well it's over now thank God.

NINA. You see, you do believe in God.

LILY. You and my father. He was forever going on about God. As long as I can remember. Do you know when my mother died he told me she'd gone to live with God? What a damn fool thing to tell a seven year old. I was furious. And so jealous. She couldn't have loved me at all, I thought, if she'd just leave me and go and live with that old man in a nighty with a long beard.

NINA (*laughing, sad*). Oh Lily . . .

LILY. My father was always saying 'God's good' or 'It's God's will' or 'God will provide'. No matter how awful things were. Even when he got senile and hardly ever knew who I was he'd be chatting away to God day and night. Well why didn't God ever tell him to get out some life insurance? Why didn't God stop him taking out that second mortgage? After he died I used to think, I'll go and find a medium . . . get a message through. 'Is this what you meant when you told me God would provide, Father? Is this it? A slummy little room that takes half my pension in rent? Not enough to eat and nobody to talk to?

NINA. Don't think about it. Don't remember it.

LILY. You're right. Silly to get worked up about it after all this time. What about one more?

NINA. I don't think I should. I've still got some here.

LILY. Well let me top it up. (*Pours again.*) No point in blaming him, really, silly old dear. He never did have any sense about money. I should have got myself some kind of job when he died. But I couldn't sort of force myself, you know Nina? I was so afraid of everything . . . all the time. Stupid.

NINA. Not stupid. You were all alone. Anyway if you had got a job you wouldn't have caught that train and we wouldn't have all been together now.

LILY (*laughs*). Well yes. Living off your husband's Life insurance in the house he did pay the mortgage on.

NINA. He'd be furious.

They both laugh. They're a bit tight.

LILY (*stops laughing. Bit bleak*). And me the parasite. Still. Always.

NINA (*indignant*). You're not! What a thing to say. We could never have managed without you. Besides there's your pension.

LILY. Just about covers the whisky. And the odd jigsaw puzzle for Gemma. (*Rather maudlin.*) I've never been any use to anyone really.

NINA. Don't be silly. I'm ashamed of you. What? All those years looking after your father and now? Look at all you do for Gemma. I would have had to put her back in the hospital if it hadn't been for you.

LILY. You never would have, Nina. You wouldn't.

NINA. I think I might have, Lily, really. I was going frantic trying to take care of her on my own. (*Pause.*) There were times when I felt like just running out of the house and never coming back. She used to frighten me so sometimes . . .

LILY. That's all over now, Nina. Drink your whisky . . .

NINA (*after a pause*). She'll be all right again in the morning won't she, Lily.

LILY. Course she will. Right as rain. It's always the same, Nina. Things build up inside her sometimes. You know. She had to . . . I don't know . . . get rid of it all some way.

NINA. But not by hurting herself. Not by cutting herself with knives and scissors and . . .

LILY. That's only happened once before.

NINA. But it could again. She might do anything, it terrifies me.

LILY. Don't think about it. You'll see. Tomorrow she'll be as bright as a button again.

NINA. Yes. I'm being silly. I think I'm a bit drunk.

LILY. You'll have to take a couple of aspirins and drink a lot of water before you go to bed. Otherwise (*Yawns.*) you'll have a hangover.

NINA. Yes, I should go to bed. (*Yawns.*) I'm too sleepy to get up out of this chair.

LILY. You have a lie in tomorrow. I'll get Gemma's breakfast.

NINA. You! Get up at Six? You won't.

LILY. Bet I will.

NINA (*sleepily*). I'll bet you five pounds.

LILY (*sleepily*). I haven't got five pounds.

They laugh comfortably together.

NINA. You know. Lily (*Yawns.*) Sometimes I wonder. If people could see the way we carry on in this house. All the games and the stories and the dressing up . . . all the things we do with Gemma, I wonder what they'd think?

LILY. They'd think we were bonkers.

NINA. I suppose we are.

LILY. Well Nina. We're not hurting anybody. As long as she's happy . . . that's all that matters. (*Yawns.*) It's my opinion . . . everybody's bonkers . . . one way . . . or . . . another . . .

NINA (*after a silence*). She's asleep. (*Yawns.*) Oh dear oh dear . . . so tired . . . must go to bed . . . must get up and . . .

Silence as they snore gently together. A clap of thunder from outside.

GEMMA (*hysterical*). Oh! Oh! Make it stop! Make it stop! Don't let them come in!

POLICEWOMAN. There, there, dear. It's only the storm. There's nobody out there. Nothing's going to hurt you.

GEMMA (*crying*). They're coming in. They are.

POLICEWOMAN. Now come along, don't be so silly. Get up. There isn't anything to hide from. (*Stern.*) Up you get now. Up. Sit in the chair. That's right. In the chair.

GEMMA *crying quietly.*

Now what's your name. Just tell me your name.

GEMMA *crying.*

We must know your name so we can find out where you live. Running about the streets crying and carrying on? We can't have that. Now tell me your name.

Clap of thunder. Louder.

NINA. What? What's that? Lily!

LILY. What is it? Nina? What's wrong?

NINA. It's a storm.

Another clap of thunder.

LILY. Gemma!

NINA. We must go up to her. She'll be so frightened. Oh quick, Lily, quick!

They get themselves up and open the door and go out into the hall. Sound of rain and wind.

LILY. Nina! The front door's open!

NINA (*frightened*). Oh Lily you don't think she's . . .

Her footsteps running upstairs.

NINA (*calling*). GEMMA! GEMMA! I'm coming darling. (*Pause. Then from upstairs.*) Lily! She's gone!

LILY. Oh dear God. Gemma! Gemma!

Out and in. GEMMA crying.

POLICEWOMAN. I can't get a thing out of her.

POLICEMAN. Never mind. They'll be here soon. The call came ten minutes ago.

POLICEWOMAN. Well who is she? Where does she come from?

POLICEMAN. Dunno. Some woman on the phone. Just asked if we'd got her. Bit hysterical.

POLICEWOMAN. She's sopping wet. Catch her death.

GEMMA (*crying*). Mummy. Mummy.

POLICEMAN. Mummy?

POLICEWOMAN. Mental case. Must be.

POLICEMAN (*loud to* GEMMA). What about a cup of tea? Like a hot cup of tea while you're waiting, eh?

GEMMA (*dangerous. Angry*). Don't touch me. Don't come near me!

POLICEMAN. All right all right, no need to shout.

GEMMA. Lily. Lily. (*Wildly.*) Where are you. Lily?

POLICEMAN. You sure she isn't drunk?

POLICEWOMAN. No I told you. She's not right in the head. (*Sharply.*) Stop that. What do you think you're doing with those chairs?

GEMMA (*breathless. Pulling chairs about*). This is my house. You can't come in here. Get away! Get away! Nobody can come in here except me and Mummy and Lily.

POLICEMAN. Oh for God's sake.

POLICEWOMAN (*warningly*). I wouldn't go near her if I were you. Look at her face. She might be dangerous.

GEMMA (*panting and banging a chair on the floor*). There! Now you can't get in. (*Then very loud, regal.*) Tell them! Tell them the new house is ready. Tell them I'm waiting. You can tell them Gemma's waiting. Go on! Go on! Get them for me! Why are you just standing there? Go! Go!

The door opens.

NINA. Gemma!

LILY. Oh look at her, Nina. Look at her.

GEMMA (*very small voice*). Mummy?

NINA (*crying*). Here we are, darling. Here we are.

   Out and in.

POLICEMAN. Gemma . . . that's with two m's is it?

LILY (*impatient*). Yes yes, that's right. Please. We must get her home.

POLICEMAN. Has to go in the book, Missus. Address?

LILY. Walnut Tree Cottage, Dene Lane.

POLICEMAN. You're her mother?

LILY. No . . . I . . . I'm not. I . . .

NINA (*from a little distance*). I'm her mother. (*To* GEMMA.) Sit there, Gemma. Just sit there quietly for a moment.

GEMMA *whimpering.*

LILY. I'll sit with her. There there, lovey. It's all right. Lily's here.

GEMMA (*whispering*). Lily did you hear them roaring and breaking the sky? Did you hear them?

LILY. They're gone now. The storm's over. They're all gone.

POLICEMAN. Age?

NINA. I beg your pardon? I don't see what . . .

POLICEMAN. How old is she . . . your daughter?

NINA. She's forty-one.

POLICEWOMAN. She lives with you, then?

NINA. Yes.

POLICEWOMAN. Seems to me she ought to be in hospital or . . . I mean she could always turn violent couldn't she. You and your friend . . . you might not be able to manage her. She's very strong isn't she.

NINA. She's always been all right with us. We take care of her. May we go now?

POLICEMAN. Well I don't know . . . well yes, I suppose you can.

NINA. Lily? Gemma?

LILY. All right, Nina. Come along, Gemma. We're going home now.

   Sound of the waves breaking.

GEMMA (*singing her tuneless song*). Can't catch me for a bumble bee. Can't catch me. Can't catch me.

End.